HOME IS WHERE THE START IS

*Ideas to Help Families
Grow in Love and Faith*

Mary Montgomery

WINSTON PRESS

Books by Mary and Herb Montgomery:
The Splendor of the Psalms
The Joy of the Psalms
Beyond Sorrow

Cover design: Terry Dugan

Scripture texts designated RSV are taken from the *Revised Standard Version Common Bible*, copyright © 1973 by the Division of Christian Education of the National Council of the Churches of Christ in the U.S.A. Used by permission. Scripture quotations designated TEV are taken from the *Good News Bible, The Bible in Today's English Version*. Copyright © American Bible Society, 1976.

"All I Wanted Was to Sing," from *Seen Through Our Eyes*, ed. Michael Gecan, is used by permission, Random House, Inc.

Copyright © 1985 by Mary Montgomery.
All rights reserved. No part of this book may be reproduced in any form without written permission from Winston Press, Inc.

Library of Congress Catalog Card Number: 84-51612

ISBN: 0-86683-868-6

Printed in the United States of America

5 4 3 2 1

Winston Press, Inc.
430 Oak Grove
Minneapolis, Minnesota 55403

To Ann, Mark, and John

Contents

Preface v
1. Deciding What You Want Home to Mean 1
2. Building Self-Esteem 10
3. Taking Time for Your Family 19
4. Listening with Your Heart 27
5. Making TV a Creative Force 34
6. Discovering the Power of Prayer 43
7. Growing into a Faith 52
8. Forgiving and Forgetting 60
9. Keeping Christ in Christmas 69
10. Giving Lent a Chance 76
11. Doing Something About Hunger 85
12. Touching with Love 92
13. Accepting Death as a Part of Life 100
14. Going Forth 110
Notes 118

Preface

Where are you on the parenting road? Just beginning the trip? Well on your way? Starting over again after a detour? When Mary had our first child twenty-one years ago, I had no idea what parenting was all about, but I had lots of strongly held theories. I still remember how seriously I discussed the burdens and responsibilities of the parenthood journey. At a neighborhood party where I was expounding my views, the mother of a large family slipped quietly in beside me. She had a sprinkling of gray in her hair, and smile lines formed around her eyes as she listened to my sober pronouncements about parenting. "You know," she said as I paused to catch my breath, "the first child gets mother's milk, the second one gets cow's milk, and the third one gets Kool-aid."

That observation has stayed with me longer than grass stains. First, because it humorously deflated my exaggerated sense of purpose. Second, because Mary and I went on to have three children. And finally, because it captures a serious truth: It takes experience to become both knowledgeable about and comfortable with family. Mary and I often reflect on how different our parental attitude would be if we had only had Ann, our first child and one who appeared to have been born with a need to cry and no need to sleep. Mark, our second child, shifted our perspective as we now learned to deal with both a girl and a boy. Then John entered our family circle, and once again our sense of what family means became larger.

My view of parenting now is best compared to what one sees in a kaleidoscope. The colorful bits and pieces of our family life are all close to me. I see that as parents and children grow older and pass through various life stages, the picture in the kaleidoscope shifts, changes, and rearranges itself but always includes something beautiful.

As a parent and writer, I'm intrigued by books and studies that reveal some supposedly new truth about raising and educating children. Although I have yet to be surprised by any finding (perhaps because I grew up in a small farming community where observing people was one of the most fascinating pastimes!), one idea sits like a star atop my tree of information. I think no one has better described what we parents do than Virginia Satir, author and pioneer in family therapy. Wherever we live, she says, is a home workshop in which we are involved in the most creative art of all—"people making." For good, or for ill, we are shaping one another!

What surprises me is that amid all the craziness that has now come out of the closet, the world is still populated with so many decent people. I cannot help but believe that God is at work and that love prevails. Although the divorce rate is high, the marriage rate is higher. Families are being formed and reformed, blended and extended. In this book—which Mary wrote and I revised—we've looked to families of all kinds to find ideas to help other families grow in love and faith.

Home *is* where the start is. The beginning of everything! The family is the basic building block out of which communities and nations are formed. Whether we blunder into parenthood or come to it after elaborate preparation, the Christian home we establish is the starting point for spiritual and moral development. From birth right on through the teen years, we parents have a major influence on our children's attitudes and beliefs and how these are put into action on an everyday basis.

In our research we came across a report that said the happiest married couples are those who have no children. We contend that many of the people who are unhappy in their family life are unhappy because they didn't know what to expect when they had children, failed to face the way they were parented themselves, and had absolutely no training in how to parent successfully.

Mary and I view home as both a nesting place and a launching pad—a nesting place in that we (parents *and* children) strive to provide a safe and secure environment for one another; a launching pad in that we (parents *and* children) try to live in a cooperative manner without a boss (or dictator!). Although Mary and I are approaching the empty nest stage, we see that experience as simply adding another detail to the kaleidoscopic picture of our ever-evolving family.

Home Is Where the Start Is is more than a book about raising children. It is a book about raising family, which only happens successfully when everyone grows. Wherever you are on your family journey, we invite you to view parenthood as a creative challenge—and most of all, a God-given opportunity.

Herb Montgomery

1

Deciding What You Want Home to Mean

Hand-me-down Upbringings

Parenting is one of the most important jobs in the world, yet it is one for which we receive virtually no formal preparation. Instead we train on the job, with a strong tendency to parent much the way we were raised. If our parents spanked and abused, the likelihood is high that we'll do the same. If they praised and encouraged us, we'll tend to be supportive and nurturing with our own children. If they were critical and fault-finding, we're likely to fall into that same pattern unless we make a determined effort to behave otherwise.

A childhood friend of mine had a mother who was big on hot breakfasts, especially in winter. This translated into oatmeal every morning. The mother's reasoning was that oatmeal warmed the stomach, which acted as a kind of furnace for the rest of the body on the walk to school. Over the years, my friend developed an aversion to oatmeal. Yet when she became a mother, she too served oatmeal to her children. Every morning! Although the kids protested, she echoed the reasoning she'd heard as a child. When I suggested there were other warm foods that could be served for breakfast, she countered, "Yes, but oatmeal's good for them." And so another generation of oatmeal-haters was created!

We need to look at our own upbringing and take from it all those practices we found nurturing: practices that made

us feel good about ourselves and said to us we were cherished members of the family. Then we need to discard the remainder of our hand-me-down upbringing and replace it with practices based on love and what seems right for our family. Two questions we might profitably ask are:
- How can I be the kind of mother or father I'd like to have for a parent?
- How can I create the kind of home I'd like to grow up in?

The answers to these questions can greatly influence the quality of our parenting and the atmosphere of our homes.

Home Is a Place Where. . . .

In the process of writing this book, I realized there are as many definitions of home as there are definers. A therapist friend told about a young man who, after working through a lot of problems with his family, said, "Home is where love is."

When I informed a three-year-old that nursery school was over and it was time to go home, she looked up at me solemn-faced. "Home," she said matter-of-factly, "is where people fight all the time."

One of our daughter's college friends with a big appetite and limited budget had quite a different perspective. "Home," he murmured, "is the place you go when you want to get full."

A fourth grader assigned to write a poem about home concluded her work with the line, "Home is where they really care when I'm not there."

What does home mean to you? And more to the point, what characterizes *your* home? Is it a place where individuals are free to be themselves, where they rightfully expect to find love and acceptance? Comfort and encouragement? There's hardly a home that measures up to our expectations all the time. But the wonder and challenge of being a parent is that we are capable of changing. What is already good can be improved upon. And if there are dark experiences of childhood we want to break with, it is possible to begin new and loving parenting patterns. Successful family life doesn't just happen, however. It's something that every family member—from the youngest to the oldest—has to work at. "Roll up your shirt sleeves," advises a family life therapist of some twenty-five years' experience. "Relating is work. Growing is work. Loving is work."

Home Is Where the Start Is

Is all the work involved in creating a nurturing home worth it? Definitely it is, because home is where the start is. It's the place where we introduce children to the values and attitudes that form their character. Traits and behavior developed early in life determine to a large extent whether a child becomes part of life's solutions or part of its problems. If we want better people to make a better world, we have to begin within the structure of the family.

Noted psychiatrist Robert Coles tells about six-year-old Ruby Bridges, whose parents instilled in her the values that sustained her while she integrated a New Orleans grade school back in 1960. As Ruby walked through crowds of hostile whites, they spit at her and called her vile names. There were even threats on her life. For months, Dr. Coles watched for signs that Ruby might be cracking under the emotional battering. Quite remarkably to him, he found no significant indications of strain. At school, Ruby studied eagerly and at home was happy in her play.

One day on her way to school, Ruby appeared to be talking to the jeering crowds. As it turned out, she was praying for them. In discussing the incident with Dr. Coles, Ruby summed it up simply by saying, "They know not what they do."

Ruby's parents were illiterate and very poor. The only way they had to protect their daughter was through the values they introduced her to at home. They taught Ruby to prize learning and entreated her to pray for those who wronged her. Carried into life, these values created a kind of stoic dignity in Ruby and gave her the emotional strength to survive an incredibly trying ordeal.[1]

Actions Speak Loudest of All

Assuredly children take on the values of their parents, but not necessarily the ones we talk about. Those they take seriously are the ones they see us living. An editorial in a small-town Oregon newspaper in 1854 suggested: "The parent who would train up a child in the way he should go, must go in the way he would train up his child."

Often children learn more from us when we're not trying to teach than when we are. Take, for example, the matter of manners. Some parents are forever reminding their children to be polite in front of company or when they are given a gift. Yet many of these same parents will bump into a child without apology or say, "Pass the pepper" or "Bring me the paper" with never so much as a "Please" or "Thank you." Unless our own manners speak for us, our words about courtesy are largely wasted.

The case for practicing what we preach is applicable to all areas of family life. Qualities such as faith, compassion, and a willingness to do something for others are likely to show themselves in children who have seen them in their parents. Adults who have a solid religious base tend to have what researchers call "high life satisfaction." That is, they are happier, more stable, and more likely to help others, according to Peter Benson of Search Institute, an organization that specializes in youth and family research. "The system of meaning that people develop—whether religious or ethical—gives life purpose and direction," Benson says. "I think the best predictor of whether you're going to have that kind of philosophy of life is having it nurtured as a child in the home."[2]

Changing Families

While Herb and I have been raising our children over the past two decades, the institution called "family" has undergone much change. We now recognize not only "traditional" families but also speak in terms of single-parent, blended, nuclear, and extended families. With the changes in family structure have come changes in the parents' roles as well. Child rearing is no longer considered just women's work. Back in 1972, Hakon Torjesen became one of the new breed known as househusbands. While his wife worked, he stayed home to care for four children. This was quite a change for a man who had spent ten years as a diplomat in the U.S. foreign service. Writing about the experience, he said, ". . . whenever we accept an opportunity for change in one area of our lives—for example in the trading of family roles—it tends to have a ripple effect that opens new choices in other areas of our living and thinking that may have seemed fixed."[3]

Although there are few full-time househusbands, many men are taking on new roles within the family structure. Increasingly, fathers are granted joint custody in divorce cases, and in many two-parent homes they are becoming more involved in the day-to-day care of their children. A lot of husbands who participate in childbirth classes with their wives report feeling a close parent-child bond right from the start. In the long run, we can expect greater involvement by fathers to be a positive influence on the family *and* on society.

Home Is an Educator

If there are parents who do not want their children to be well educated, I have never met one. Education is recognized as the entree to respectability and success, and many parents make substantial sacrifices to see that their children get the proper schooling. But an international study has confirmed that schools are not the most important factor in a child's educational achievement. A study that involved 300 experts, 250,000 students, 50,000 teachers, and 20 countries found that although schools do make a difference, the home background is even more important.[4]

In homes where parents take education seriously, there is a high probability that their children will do likewise.

Where parents do not, schools can't be expected to stimulate a desire to learn. That is not to say that parents should formally teach young children academic skills but rather that home should be a place where learning is prized. "Parents who love learning will create a stimulating environment for children, which is far more beneficial to them than specific instruction," maintains child psychologist David Elkind. "Parents who fill the house with books, paintings and music, who have interesting friends and discussions, who are curious and ask questions provide young children with all the intellectual stimulation they need. In such an environment, formal instruction would be like ordering a hamburger at a four-star restaurant."[5]

We Can't Afford It

Not surprisingly, a financial squeeze is one of the most persistent stresses on families. As divorce increases, more and more mothers have to join the work force. Even in two-parent households, having both parents work outside the home is more the norm than the exception. In some homes where both parents puruse careers, money is secondary to the fulfillment their jobs provide. In more and more cases, however, it takes two paychecks to ensure the family's financial survival. If home is to be a harmonious place, a consensus has to be reached both on how money is earned and how it is to be spent. That holds true whether there is a little of it or a lot.

Children pick up attitudes about money even before they know how to use it. Researchers say what while children are still toddlers, their parents' feelings about money form the children's attitudes toward it. Do we fight over money? Use it to buy material goods that become a substitute for love? Spend first and save what's left, or the other way around?

It's easy in our consumer society to feel guilty about those things we are not giving our children—the toy that "everybody" has or the designer label that seems so important. In a home where there is an abundance of love, children are not likely to suffer greatly because of what we cannot buy them. They might, in fact, benefit. Author and parent Morris Mandel writes:

> Four magic words, *we can't afford it,* should be a part of every child's education. A child who has never heard these words—or also has never been forced to abide by their meaning—has surely been cheated by his parents. As exercise strengthens the body, frugality strengthens the spirit. Without its occasional discipline, character suffers.[6]

Traditions Make Us Unique

All families have traditions, and each new family becomes a melding of the traditions that two partners bring to it. Our traditions set us apart as a unique group of people with our own ways of doing things. One family opens presents on Christmas Eve, another on Christmas morning. One family always goes to Grandma's house for Thanksgiving. Another stays home and has the grandparents as guests. There might be a tradition of always putting the birthday cake on a special plate or of having grilled cheese sandwiches on Sunday evening. Traditions create a feeling of family closeness and give children a sense of heritage that helps them feel secure.

Sometimes we need to do a housecleaning of our traditions. Going to the grandparents' place for an annual Thanksgiving dinner might be fine for a while, but when circumstances change we should be flexible. Maybe the most important thing becomes staying home and developing traditions that one day might be carried on in our children's homes.

In our family, we decided that when one tradition is uprooted, another should be planted. In a sense it's a bit like reforesting. The practice we start today grows into the tradition of tomorrow, taking its place alongside others we choose to keep alive in an effort to create a home that will be remembered with warmth.

Some Things to Try

- Divide a sheet of paper into two parts and list both the good and the bad parenting you experienced as a child. If you live in a two-parent family, share your list with your spouse and discuss how you want to parent your children. Commit yourself to discarding hurtful practices.
- Forgive your parents and other adults for mistakes you feel they made in raising you. Seek God's forgiveness for any grudges you hold against your parents. Through forgiving and being forgiven, we open ourselves up to be more loving.
- Begin a family scrapbook or update one that has been started. Include photos, clippings, postcards—anything that holds significance for the family and keeps memories alive. Remember to date pictures and name the people in them. Do the same with clippings and other memorabilia. This is especially helpful when scrapbooks pass from one generation to the next.
- Create a scrapbook for each child. We save school pictures, report cards, handmade greeting cards, artwork, stories, cards from camp, and anything else that is a part of our children's history. When they graduate from high school, they receive a scrapbook filled with what we have collected. To have such a "life story" in hand is a very affirming experience.
- Help children become wise money managers. About the time our children started school, we began giving them small weekly allowances. Later, we switched to paying it once a month and found that this gave them more money-managing experience. They quickly discovered that being a big spender the first week left them with empty pockets the rest of the month. We reviewed allowance about twice a year and tried to determine what the children were expected to spend their money on and what we would

help out with. It's amazing how much consideration children will give a purchase when it's their own money they're spending! When ours reached their mid-teens and were earning money, we stopped giving allowances.
- Read *Traits of a Healthy Family* by Dolores Curran (Winston Press). This is a practical and highly readable book about the qualities of healthy families that produce healthy people.

2

Building Self-Esteem

Through the Eyes of Others

Our son Mark was still a preschooler when he snuggled in my lap and confided with great seriousness, "I like me better when Ann likes me." Ann is Mark's sister, older by two and a half years, and her approval of him was obviously important. But Mark's feelings underscored a larger truth. That is, young children see themselves very much the way their family and others who play important roles in their lives see them. If we make them feel attractive, bright, and lovable, that is the way they see themselves. On the contrary, if our words and actions make them feel ugly or stupid, their sense of worth is diminished. *Home is the starting place for building self-esteem.* It's where we have countless opportunities to help children feel good about who they are and to alert them to the possibilities of what they can become.

A friend recalls that her positive self-image was formed in large part by her father, who always referred to their family of girls as his "five beautiful daughters." Yet when this friend looks back at old picture albums, she realizes that beauty is in the eye of the beholder. "In my teen years I was gangly as a rope," she now admits. "I had frizzed permanents and a smile that showed off a mouthful of braces. But through it all I don't remember thinking of myself as unattractive, and I'm sure my dad's attention and love had a lot to do with it. He made me think not only that I was lovely but that I could do anything I set my mind to." In the years since, she has been an achiever, a person with a strong sense of who she is and what she wants in life.

The Most Valuable Psychological Possession

Think for a moment about people you know who are confident and have a vital sense of purpose. Almost certainly you will discover that they have a high degree of self-esteem, a word the dictionary defines as "confidence and satisfaction with oneself." People with high self-esteem are survivors. Like everyone else, they are prey to disappointment and failure, but they tend to have the inner strength to live through crises and be strengthened by them. Quite the reverse is true of those with low self-esteem. They are notably poor in handling problems and pressures. Counselors voice a common observation: kids who get caught up in problems of drug abuse and delinquency almost invariably suffer from low self-esteem. Young people who feel okay about themselves are more likely to follow their own beliefs. The fact that others are getting into trouble doesn't mean they have to.

Clearly a good self-image is the most valuable psychological possession anyone can have. So how do we give our children this valued possession? How do we help them feel like worthy people able to face life with dignity and confidence?

Love That's Unconditional

Basic to a good self-image is letting children know we love them as they are. If we have a boy, we do not wish he had been born a girl, or the other way around. If a child is shy, we do not lament that she is not more outgoing. If a boy is short, we do not regret that he is not tall. Beyond this, children need to know there are no strings attached to our love: that we love them when they're acting up as well as when they behave; when they're crabby as well as when they're friendly.

Too frequently children get the message, both spoken and unspoken, that their worth is contingent upon staying out of trouble, being neat, doing well in school or music or sports, or an endless list of those things that tend to make parents proud. "If they [children] perceive only conditional love, which will be withdrawn as soon as they stop fulfilling the imposed conditions, they will perceive themselves as worthless. They will feel 'used,'" states John Powell, whose writing draws upon his experiences as a teacher and counselor. "The emotional response to this conditional love will probably be a blend of anger, insecurity, and a strong need for approval."[1]

Yet another damaging aspect of conditional love is that it fails to prepare children to understand the God of *un*conditional love. This is a God who loves them in spite of their shortcomings and failings; who loves them not because of how they look or for what they accomplish but simply because they are. The best way for children to know such a God is to have experienced unconditional love at home.

The love out of which self-esteem grows has nothing to do with social class or economic status. Indeed, a beautiful home can be love impoverished and a modest one can be an environment that builds self-esteem. Looking back at her childhood, one mother recalled,

> The climate in our home was always that you could be anything you wanted to be. "Keep your eyes on the stars and your feet on the ground" was a family slogan. No adversity could keep us from our goals. We were urged to think of our options. My mother taught us that it's not important what one has, only how one feels. Though we lived in a tenement, we never felt poor. We were rich in spirit, ability, caring, and laughter.[2]

Beware of Comparisons

Although home is the place where the foundations of self-esteem are laid, comparisons can knock out the underpinnings. "Your sister isn't always spilling *her* milk; what's wrong with you?" "Your brother gets As on his report card, but I never see any on yours." "Johnny Ambitious has a paper route. Why don't you get a job and earn some money?" Such statements may be made with the intention of motivating a child, but the message that comes across is "You don't measure up. You're inferior." Aside from damaging self-esteem, comparisons are destructive in that they foster undue resentment among brothers and sisters. Although some sibling rivalry is natural, it can become intense and anger-filled when parents compare one child with another.

On the other hand, self-esteem is enhanced if we deal with matters directly and positively. For the chronic milk-spiller we might serve milk in a sturdy mug that's less likely to get knocked over. The child feels less like a klutz, and we won't have to deal with as many spills. When a report card is an issue, we should use sensitivity and tact to find out if there's a problem with a particular subject or a particular teacher. If all seems in order, perhaps setting an earlier bedtime or scheduling more time on homework will lead to better performance.

Finally, we have to accept the uniqueness of each child. One may be the family scholar, another the tinkerer who can take anything apart and put it back together; one may be interested in music, another in cooking. Rather than being critical of the qualities children lack and what they cannot do, how much better to focus on what is special about them and what they *can* do.

Today's children are pressured to excel at an ever-earlier age and to do so academically, socially, athletically. Often young people who feel they don't measure up seek escape in drugs or religious movements. "Indeed, the great appeal of many of the charismatic religious groups is that when young people join, they are assured that support is *not* contingent upon achievement," writes child psychologist David Elkind, who laments the pressures on today's children to grow up too fast.[3] What a lot of problems and heartache could be avoided if children felt they were loved and accepted for who they are and not for how they check out compared with someone else.

Let Individuals Be Individual

Our two sons are only a year apart in school. When they were in the elementary grades, teachers often remarked, "It's hard to believe they're brothers. They're so different from each other." This comment always left me nonplussed. "Why *shouldn't* they be different?" I wondered. Because they were brothers, did it mean they should both be like the older one, gregarious and sports-loving? Or should the older be like his less-social younger brother who avidly collected stamps and wrote delightfully imaginative stories? Trying to make one child be like another can be futile and destructive. God created each child a distinct and separate individual, unlike anyone who has ever been or ever will be. Much of the wonder and joy in raising children lies in recognizing their uniqueness and celebrating it.

Anything that gives a child "I-can-do" feelings bolsters self-esteem. The more interests children have and the more abilities they develop, the better they will tend to feel about themselves. Depending upon the child's age, confidence-building activities might be building with blocks or painting a picture, creating a puppet or making pudding, playing a musical instrument or learning to swim, acting in a play or going out for basketball. "When kids feel good about what they can do, they're better able to tolerate the anxieties that growing up involves," states educator Dr. Thomas Lickona. "They have less need to seek security through conformity or to escape through drugs, drinking, or sex."[4]

With the issue of sexism now part of the public consciousness, there is somewhat less stereotyping of activities as suitably male or female. Granted, we still have a long way to go, but a start has been made. Girls now have more opportunities to participate in sports, and boys who have an interest in cooking or the arts are less likely to be labeled effeminate. There is no better place to begin stamping out sexism than at home. Having a boy and a girl in the family should not mean that the girl does the household chores because it's "women's work." The message to boys is that women exist to care for them, and to girls that it's their lot in life to clean up after someone else.

Praise Is a Two-edged Sword

There's a Dennis the Menace cartoon in which Dennis, sitting in his rocking chair facing a corner, glances at the departing back of his mother. "How come I don't have a special place to sit when I do somethin' *nice*?" reads the caption. How much more readily we criticize and punish than affirm and congratulate! Yet there's hardly a person among us, child or adult, who doesn't enjoy being recognized for doing something well. Although praise helps us form a good opinion of ourselves and feel kindly toward others it's a two-edged sword. Used inadvisedly, it can be as harmful as it is helpful.

Haim Ginott was one of the first specialists to analyze the uses of praise. He gives examples of praise that is helpful and praise that is not.

> *Helpful praise:* I liked your get-well card. It was so pretty and witty.
> *Possible inference:* I have good taste, I can rely on my choices.
> (*Unhelpful praise:* You are *always* so considerate.)
> *Helpful praise:* Thanks for telling me that I overpaid you. I appreciate it very much.
> *Possible inference:* I'm glad I was honest.
> (*Unhelpful praise:* You are such an honest child.)[5]

All of us, children included, know that we are not *always* considerate and can probably recall times when we were less than honest. However well intended, praise that makes exaggerated claims leads to embarrassment and discomfort on the part of the one being extolled. *If praise is to work toward the desired end of building self-esteem, it needs to be realistic and focused on the matter at hand.* The following principles of praise are effective with adults and children alike: Recognize the human need for praise, look for what is praiseworthy, compliment sincerely.

Curtailing Competition

For young children, much of life is still possibility. They need time to explore and discover, to fail and try again before being pitted in contests, one against the other. For the sake of building self-esteem it would be ideal to hold competitiveness to a minimum in the early years. How many children loved to draw and paint until the "best" work was displayed on the bulletin board and theirs wasn't included? How many children ran and played for the sheer pleasure of being active, but got involved in organized sports and spent most of their time on the bench because they didn't have the skills to help the team win? Even children who are deemed "best" have trouble with competition as expressed by Mary Wilke in her poem "All I Wanted Was to Sing":

> When I was in first grade I loved to sing.
> When it was my turn I'd stand up clearly and
>   happily, thoroughly enjoying myself.
> My teacher declared me singing champion. . . .
>
> Why did something as innocent and joyful as the
>   music of small children have to be turned into a
>   contest?
> The voices should have been sources of joy, not
>   pride or shame.
> But my first grade teacher thought that my talent
>   should be brandished in front of my peers. . . .
>
> My joy became a mixture of pride and shame and
>   as time went on shame overshadowed
>   pride. . . .

My teacher was the one who wanted a champion;
All I wanted was to sing.[6]

Sandbox play, tree climbing, fort building, exploring, exercising—all are ways that young children can be active and interact with one another without having to be winners or losers. Opportunities to play cooperatively and to test their abilities without the pressure of competition help children feel good about themselves. What could be better preparation for life and its competitiveness than a healthy sense of self-worth?

Quite a Bargain

Although we may let our children know through words and actions that they are bright, beautiful, and wonderful, early on they encounter forces that chip away at their self-esteem. Other people don't think they are quite as special as we do. Inevitably, children compare themselves to their peers and, in comparison, feel like something less than extraordinary. A time also comes when the opinion of others is more important to them than ours. If we compliment a fifteen-year-old, we might hear, "You have to say that. You're my parent." Even when children don't put a lot of stock in our opinions, they want to know they are cherished and valued. Whatever we can do to give this feeling is a gift beyond measure because it forms the bedrock of their self-esteem.

Educator and speaker Dr. Lillian Katz tells of her son who once informed her that he'd read in the newspaper it cost $65,000 to raise a child from birth to age eighteen.

After considering the information for a moment, she said, "For someone as infinitely precious as you, I think that's quite a bargain."

"You always have your own twist to put on things," her son replied.[7] And what a nice twist it was!

Some Things to Try

- Never do for children what they can do for themselves. As a toddler tries to button a coat, it's tempting to say, "Let me

help," or as a ten-year-old awkwardly frosts a cake, we're inclined to say, "I'll do that for you." If we do for them what they can learn to do for themselves, we deny them experiences that build self-reliance and self-esteem.
- Begin early to display children's artwork and craft projects. In our house, we had the GE Art Gallery—a refrigerator that for years provided display space for paintings and drawings. Remember that relatives, especially grandparents, enjoy getting children's artwork and crafts as gifts.
- Call children by the names they prefer. It's unkind to persist in calling a daughter Betty Lou when she wants to be known as Betty or a boy "Skipper" when he loathes the nickname.
- When reprimanding children, do it in private whenever possible. Being corrected in front of others is humiliating and hard on self-esteem.
- Encourage children to set goals for themselves. The goal can be anything from saving to buy a toy to finishing a book. In setting goals, the child is saying, "I am a person who can do what I set my mind on."
- Read *Self-Esteem: A Family Affair* by Jean Illsley Clarke (Winston Press). The book promotes the idea that a child's needs are best met by grown-ups whose needs are met. It is designed to bring out the best in parents and their children.

3

Taking Time for Your Family

The Gift of Ourselves

When children stand no taller than your knee, it's hard to imagine they'll ever be grown up. When they are, it's difficult to remember them as curious toddlers or fifth graders struggling with long division or even as teens, smiling in triumph after passing their driver's test. In retrospect, the years of raising children pass quickly. But when we're in the midst of them, there's a tendency to think we'll always have a tomorrow in which to do those things we don't get around to today—simple things like reading to a child or visiting the zoo, taking a leisurely walk or going fishing.

Scripture reminds us that "For everything there is a season, a time for every matter under heaven" (Ecclesiastes 3:1, RSV). The season for giving the gift of ourselves is now. If we do, we won't look back with regret and wonder where all the years went because there were so many things we planned to do with our families . . . when we had the time.

Rich or poor, young or old, we all get the same number of hours each day. Although we may say we are going to "make time" to do something, it isn't possible. We can only *take the time* from our daily allotment of twenty-four hours. Time might be thought of as a commodity that needs to be budgeted much the same way we budget money. With both, we have some fixed commitments, but beyond that we make our own decisions.

Although time spent with the family has the potential for paying dividends in personal closeness, it does not guarantee it. Warm, durable relationships do not automatically result because family members spend time together. A counselor who works with troubled teens says they speak of "mothers and fathers who had been around the house for years, but whom they had never met. . . . They described parents who never looked into their eyes, and parents who lost the art of living in love."[1] In the time that we do spend with our families, we need to be really present to one another, listening, affirming, and trying our best to understand what it's like to be that other person.

Never Too Late

Many of us realize the importance of spending time with children only when it seems too late. The years have slipped away, and with them our good intentions. It's possible to reach out at any age but as children get older, finding ways to spend time together may require creative thinking such as fifteen-year-old Patrick describes.

When asked to submit an essay about his favorite toy, Patrick wrote about the golf clubs his father gave him on his eleventh birthday. He explained that his father traveled a lot and that when they saw one another—which was seldom—their conversation consisted mostly of small talk. But after Patrick got the clubs, he and his father began playing golf together every Sunday. "Anyone spending three hours of non-stop togetherness a week has to get beyond small talk, and we did," Patrick wrote. "As it became easier for my father and me to convey our thoughts to each other, our relationship strengthened, helping us through the happy times as well as the sad."[2]

It's easy to get so caught up in earning a living that we find ourselves spending less and less time with our families. Typically, this has been the case with fathers. However, now that some sixty percent of American women with children under eighteen work outside the home,[3] it's becoming true of mothers as well. Yet if we make spending time together a priority, it's amazing how ingenious we can be about getting the most out of each day and how wisely we can invest our energies.

Sharing Books

Few activities create a warmer bond between parent and child than sitting close and reading a book. Interest in books begins early. About the time children reach their first birthday, they enjoy looking at pictures when nursery rhymes are read or sung to them. By a year and a half or two years, they often like to turn the pages themselves and know the words so well that they correct even the slightest change in script. As children get older, being read to provides the opportunity for them to ask questions and express ideas. We in turn are included in their world of awakening interests. Once children are hooked on books, it's an open road to shared enjoyment for years to come.

If a regular time for reading aloud is scheduled, children come to anticipate it much the way we look forward to lunch with a friend. Two possibilities for storytime are before naps and before the child's bedtime. Once we discover how mutually enriching storytime is, even the busiest schedule can be made to accommodate it.

As children become readers themselves, our tendency is to stop reading to them. This is unfortunate because sharing books provides opportunities to communicate about topics that might not otherwise come up. One mother relates how, after reading a particularly moving true story, she felt compelled to read it to her family. This touched off the family's after-dinner read-alouds. They followed the escapades of Robin Hood, rafted down the Mississippi with Huck and Jim, got swept up in the adventures of castaways in *Mysterious Island*. Family members took turns reading. One son who was a poor reader increased his skill significantly. "Reading together has given us a good measuring stick," says the mother. "We can more easily compare values, and ask ourselves, 'What is truly satisfying?

Really important?' We feel we have gained a broader respect for others and their ways."[4]

Even in homes where books aren't read aloud, there always seems to be something to talk about in a family of readers. Information gleaned from a newspaper or magazine is passed along or the plot of a book is discussed. There's hardly a person of any age who won't become talkative when asked about something he or she is reading.

Scheduling Family Time

Some families set aside a block of time to spend with one another every day. Most often this is at a meal. Other families plan a once-a-week family night. It's a time away from schedules, neighbors, and friends; a time to talk together, to play, and pray. Such enjoyable experiences create warm memories and establish traditions.

A family with three young teens discovered that what they did on family night was less important than the sharing of time with one another. They began by reading prayers or Scripture in keeping with the liturgical season and followed up with a variety of activities. They've sat around talking to one another, written letters to a grandma living in a distant state, visited the nearby science museum, attended a movie, and sometimes just gone out for hamburgers.

Are family nights always entered into with enthusiasm? Is the time spent together always a peaceful interlude marked by sensitivity and caring? Hardly. Kids complain about missing favorite TV shows. Parents face awkward moments, and sometimes the planned activities fizzle. But those times are outnumbered by the good things that happen. The time together fosters a feeling of community within the family, and members gain insights into themselves and one another. Perhaps the most important benefit is that they laugh and have fun together. It happens because they have taken time to enjoy one another's company.

If family time is begun when children are young, there are fewer schedule conflicts and it's easier to get together on a regular basis. Some families set aside Sunday as their day. One family with two children in grade school settled on Tuesday evening as their night. "There are times when I'm really tired and would like to be doing other things," the father admits. "But I think playing Monopoly or going on a picnic or whatever we do as a family is far more important. The time we've spent together has paid off for all of us."

Some families don't set aside a specific time but manage to be together on a flexible basis. In a family with several young children, the general rule is that each child gets one outing a week alone with a parent. It might involve getting an ice cream cone or taking a walk. Then again it might just be going to the hardware store on an errand. The important thing is getting their "alone time" each week.

In a family where both parents work, the children like to schedule time by making appointments in their parents' datebooks. "This seemed silly to me at first," the mother says, "but the kids like doing it—and do it often. It seems to say to them that they are as important as any business engagement—and they certainly are."

Working Together

Sharing household jobs is a good way for families to come to appreciate one another. When our dishwasher sputtered its final spray, each child was assigned turns drying the dishes while a parent washed. Although it was a job none of us was joyous about doing, it did give us the chance to talk. In the course of getting the job done, we heard about new friendships and found out about broken ones; we learned about a fondness for a particular teacher and the dislike of another one; we discussed a successfully completed report and shared fears about standing in front of a group to give a report. Even after the dishwasher was replaced with a new one, we continued to hand wash when there weren't enough dishes for a full load. The sharing that went on was a benefit too good to give up.

Some of our working together has been on one-time projects. A garage sale was a cooperative effort that resulted in fun as well as some extra "family money." And once when our house seemed to have a hundred things in need of paint, repair, or cleaning, we spent the day working on projects and marking them off a long list. As we literally put our house in order, we shared in the pride of accomplishment.

The Father Factor

Although today's fathers are taking over more roles traditionally held by women, in many families it's still Mom who does the bulk of the parenting. So is it really important if Dad goes to school conferences and takes the children to the park or just out for a walk? According to a continuing survey by the National Children's Bureau in London, the answer appears to be yes, the involvement of fathers is very important.

The study, which is monitoring 16,000 British children from birth through early life and schooling, found that children whose fathers came to school conferences and accompanied them on outings did measurably better in school. That is not to say that if a father spends an afternoon with his child, the child will automatically spell or add better. What the study does reveal is that when fathers accompanied the mothers to school meetings, the children scored as much as seven months higher in reading and mathematics assessment tests than children whose mothers went alone. Said the research officer:

> It's not just the actual number of times the father goes to school with the mother or takes his child out. But these are considered to be the most important things affecting a child's score. They are symptomatic of an overall attitude of caring. . . . No matter what kind of financial situation or family size a child comes from,

the father's active participation made a definite difference to the child's progress.[5]

We Can Say More than "Oh!"

It isn't just the children who gain from time spent with parents. In looking back at his years of child-rearing, a father commented, "I used to consider the time I spent with my kids to be for their benefit. But now I realize it was a chance for both generations to learn and have a good time."

Another father looks back at what he would do if his child were small again and writes, "I would stop reading the newspaper when he wants to talk with me. I would try to refrain from words of impatience at the interruption. Such times can be the best times to show love and kindness." He goes on to make his point about giving children attention by telling of a small boy who tried to show his father a scratch on his finger. After repeated attempts to gain his father's attention, the father stopped reading and said impatiently, "Well, I can't do anything about it, can I?"

"Yes, Daddy," his small son said. "You could have said, 'Oh.'"[6]

Indeed, any one of us can say "Oh" . . . and more. All we need do is take the time.

Some Things to Try

- Get family members to commit themselves to a family night once a week for a month. Work together to plan an activity for each evening. Do the things you've always thought about doing but have never taken the time for.
- Use mealtimes as an opportunity to be together as a family. It's a chance to share ideas and exchange the experiences of the day. Everyone should be recognized and made to feel that what he or she has to contribute is important to the conversation. When children reach their teen years, jobs and school activities have a way of encroaching on the dinner hour, but there are almost

always some nights during the week when the family can be together.
- Seek a mutual interest for at least two family members to share. The interest will, of course, depend upon the ages of the children. Some families experience togetherness in such pursuits as making banners, writing computer programs, or being part of a cause such as the pro-life or peace movements. Activities such as cooking or sewing or woodworking can be shared interests for a parent and child. When one of our children was in the intermediate grades, he developed an interest in coins and stamps. The collections his dad had started as a child gave him a good start, and over a period of years they went off together to many stamp and coin shows.
- Read the *Read-Aloud Handbook* by James Trelease. The book suggests practical ways to inspire children to develop the habit of reading. It also lists hundreds of books appropriate for children of all ages.
- Have a variety of games for indoor and outdoor play. These do not have to be expensive. Hours of enjoyment can be had from a frisbee, a bat and ball, a checkerboard, or various card games. Activities need to change as children grow in age and skill; however, much of the same equipment can be used and many of the same games played for years. It is simply a matter of bringing a higher level of skill to them.
- Plan vacations that promote togetherness. A friend was raised in a family that made do on very little money. Yet no matter how meager the family income, they always managed to put aside enough for a fishing trip in a neighboring state. It meant staying in a rustic cabin at a lake where they spent their days fishing and swimming and at night having a fish dinner from the catch of the day. In the evening they amused themselves playing cards and having popcorn and homemade fudge. Although the children are grown now, those trips are among their most treasured memories of family life.

4

Listening with Your Heart

The Need to Be Listened To

When we have someone who will listen to our problems, the solutions often become obvious and advice is not needed. A psychiatrist friend admits she would lose a good portion of her business if her clients had even one person who was a good listener—someone in whom they could confide honestly and who would not be judgmental. That is not to discount the importance of professional counseling. For adults and children alike, there are instances when such counseling is necessary. But in many cases, all we need to get us through troublesome times is a good listener.

A counselor makes this point when he tells about being asked to sit in with some mothers who were sharing complaints. A few minutes into the session, he realized that psychology and counseling weren't what was called for. Rather, the women simply needed to talk among themselves. After they had sympathized, empathized, and shed an occasional tear, they ended up laughing at the frustrations of family life. "They thanked me for coming over and being so helpful," said the counselor. "I realized as I walked away that they were thanking me for listening and for saying nothing."[1]

Sometimes good listening requires that we be quiet, other times that we respond. Knowing when to do which means we must listen not just with our ears but with our hearts as well.

Half of any conversation is listening. When we listen, we show our respect for the one who is talking and affirm his or her self-worth. But sometimes in dealing with children, we suspend the rules of good communication. Instead of talking *with* children, we talk *to* them or *at* them. Describing an exchange with a parent, a young boy said, "My dad and I had words this morning, but I didn't get to use mine."

Home is the place where listening habits are formed. If we don't listen to our children, we can hardly expect them to listen to us.

A Skill That Can Be Learned

Hearing is something we do passively, but listening is a skill that requires attention and mental effort. Like any other skill, it can be learned. The fact that we have not listened well in the past does not mean that we cannot be better listeners tomorrow.

A good listener takes an interest in the person who is speaking—and shows it. When we give our full attention, we are in effect saying, "You are worthy of my time. You are someone worth listening to." Developing eye contact shows we are listening. So, too, does sitting or standing attentively and looking interested. When we're communicating with small children, attentive listening often involves sitting, bending, or kneeling to put ourselves on their eye level.

Being a good listener also requires that we try to put ourselves in the other person's place. What is it like to be the wife who says she feels rejected, or the husband who says he feels unappreciated? How does it feel to be a five-year-old who comes home in tears and says, "Billy doesn't like me anymore," or to be an adolescent who complains, "You don't trust me"? If we're sensitive listeners, we'll hear not just the words but the feelings behind them. Getting feelings out in the open is crucial to good family communication.

The communication channels are kept open when we let the other person know our interpretation of what has been said. It might be with a comment such as "I understand you to say you think you're being treated unfairly" or "What I hear you saying is that you think the rule should be changed." Remember, if you can't play back what the other person has just said, you haven't been listening.

Communication is limited if we listen only to what's complimentary and agreeable. When we're committed to being a good listener, we won't get defensive, or worse yet, cut off communication if the words become accusatory. Rather, we hear the other person out, and in doing so hope to gain insights that will give us a better understanding of the situation.

Questions, Questions, Questions

Children are no different from adults in that they want to be listened to respectfully and have their questions taken seriously. Although questions such as Why don't clouds fall down? or How come grass is green instead of blue? may seem absurd to us, they are not to the child. When we cannot answer a question, we can still dignify a child's asking it by admitting "I don't know." If the question seems worth pursuing, we might suggest trying to find out the answer together, and then follow up by looking in a book or asking someone who would know.

Children ask questions at the moment they occur to them, and often their timing couldn't be worse. Just when there is something boiling over on the stove, they want to know what makes it thunder, and just as the phone rings, they ask how babies get born. If we can't take time for a child's question, we can show we've been listening by saying, "I can't answer now. We'll talk about it later." Then be sure to do so. In answering questions, remember that children don't want to know everything we know. What they are after is information they can absorb and fit into the knowledge they already have. A little girl who asked her father how she was put together got an explanation about conception and birth. When he finished, she said, "No, no. I meant, how does your head stay on?"

In answering children's questions, it's important to be brief, to explain simply, and to keep on track by asking, "Does that answer your question?" or "Is that what you wanted to know?" When the door for further discussion is left ajar, children feel free to come back when they're ready for more information or curious about another topic.

Listening to Body Language and Behavior

Effective listening involves being aware of body signals as well as words. A shrug, a smile, a nervous laugh, gestures, facial expressions, and posture speak for themselves. When Maria comes home from school with slumped shoulders and dragging footsteps, she doesn't have to tell us she's unhappy. A comment such as "It looks like something has gone wrong for you," might encourage Maria to share her feelings. But if no response is forthcoming, it's best not to pursue the matter. "It is important not to try to force the child to share his or her feelings," state Drs. Dinkmeyer and McKay in their handbook for effective parenting. "There will be many opportunities to try again, if you make attempts to respond to the child's invitations."[2]

Children at play reveal a great deal about how they perceive their world. If you've ever listened to your child talking on a toy telephone, you may have been amazed and perhaps a bit dismayed at how much the tone of voice and mannerisms resembled yours. Children who are stern when taking on the role of adults—perhaps spanking their dolls when playing house—are probably treated harshly themselves. Older children who bully younger ones might only be passing along the treatment that has been meted out to them.

A Matter of Life and Death

Listening to words and behavior is so important that it can literally be a matter of life or death. Although the possibility that anyone you know will take his or her own life may seem remote, suicide is the third leading cause of death among youths between the ages of ten and nineteen. Increasingly, even children of five and six are ending their own lives.[3]

A comprehensive treatment of suicide is well beyond the scope of this chapter, but a discussion on listening would be incomplete without reference to the importance of being alert to signs that someone is suicidal. Among the clues in behavior are sleep disorders, prolonged depression, exaggerated mood swings, unexplainable exhaustion, and accidents that have the potential for causing serious injury.

It is commonly believed that people who talk about suicide don't really do it. This is simply not true.

> Before committing suicide, people often make direct statements about their intention to end their lives, or less direct comments about how they might as well be dead or that their friends and family would be better off without them. Suicide threats and similar statements should always be taken seriously. They are a real sign of danger.[4]

Another common belief is that if you ask someone if he or she is thinking about suicide, you may be giving them the idea. Professionals who work with the suicidal generally agree that if the behavior that suggests suicide is there, the idea is also there. The person may be waiting to be asked; then we need to be ready to listen without moralizing or passing judgment. Scripture captures the poignance of this situation well when it states, "If you will not listen, my soul will weep in secret. . ." (Jeremiah 13:17, RSV).

A Gift Beyond Price

Once we have acquired the art of listening, it becomes a gift that is ours to give. The gift of listening can be given to anyone at any time, and it costs us nothing but our time and interest. Yet to our families and others who need a listener, it is a gift beyond price. No matter what our listening habits have been in the past, each of us can start today to be a better listener, one who hears with the ears and listens with the heart.

Some Things to Try

- Take young children for walks and listen to the sounds of nature. Do this throughout the year because the seasons have sounds of their own. Listen for the wind, the rustle of leaves, the crunch of snow underfoot, the song of a bird, the chirp of crickets, the bark of a dog. An appreciation for the wonders of nature builds an awareness of the God who created it all and gave us eyes that we might see and ears that we might hear.
- Listen to your tone of voice, especially when speaking to family members. Objectively try to determine if it's harsh, friendly, whining, gruff, overbearing, loving, monotonous, cheerful. Tone of voice communicates more surely than the words spoken.
- Record and send tapes to relatives and friends. Encourage children to tell about their lives and perhaps to read or recite a short poem they would like to share. This is an especially good way to keep in touch when children are too young to write letters. When grandparents can't be at birthday parties, one family puts a tape recorder on the table and sends them a recording of the mealtime conversation.
- If you have young children and your work requires that you are frequently away from home, record yourself reading some of your child's favorite stories. Listening to such tapes can be a great comfort to a child during a parent's absence.
- As a family, pray for the ability to listen well. Perhaps you will want to copy this prayer and put it where everyone at home will see it.

> Teach me to listen, Lord,
>   to those nearest me,
>   my family, my friends, my co-workers.

Help me to be aware that no matter what words
    I hear,
the message is,
"Accept the person I am. Listen to me."
Teach me to listen, Lord,
    to those far from me—
    the whisper of the hopeless,
    the plea of the forgotten,
    the cry of the anguished.
Teach me to listen, Lord,
    to myself.
    Help me to be less afraid,
    to trust the voice inside—
    in the deepest part of me.
Teach me to listen, Lord,
    for Your voice—
    in busyness and in boredom,
    in certainty and in doubt,
    in noise and in silence.
Teach me, Lord, to listen.
        Amen.[5]

5

Making TV a Creative Force

A Major Influence

Of all the innovations in this century, television is among the most widely used and accepted. Over 70 percent of homes in the U.S.—some 58 million—have a television set.[1] On average, adults spend 80 percent of their leisure time watching TV, and the average child spends 26 hours per week in front of the magic box.[2] By the time a child graduates from high school, he or she will have spent 15,000 hours viewing television and only 12,000 hours in the classroom. When questioned in a national poll, the majority of junior high students said that television had a greater influence on their lives than books, radio, newspapers, or magazines.[3]

Television has become a major force in shaping children's lives. Even its fiercest critics admit that when television is good it can be very, very good. It opens windows to other worlds and shows us important events happening half a world away, or even on the moon. But all too frequently the medium serves up mediocre fare or worse, and every social ill from low reading scores to increased crime has been laid at its electronic doorstep.

The Negative Impact

Television violence, like the weather, is one of those things a lot of people discuss but no one does anything about. Police shows perennially make up 30 percent of prime time TV. Although these programs are created for an adult audience, Nielsen statistics show that children aged 6 to 11 do 30 percent of their TV viewing during prime time hours.[4]

Does watching TV violence increase violent behavior? The answer depends on which expert you listen to. Some say it does not. Others contend that after watching a lot of physical and psychological violence, viewers of all ages become so inured to it that they more readily tolerate violence in real life. Several studies have shown that after watching violence on TV, children become more aggressive. Commenting on a study conducted over a 5-year period among 10,000 children ages 8-13, a reporter wrote, "Just because a youngster sees a bank robbery on a cop show doesn't mean he will run out and stick up the local pizza parlor. But violence on screen does breed an inclination toward aggression off screen."[5]

Violence depicted on television is being supplemented by more emphasis on sex. Rival networks play the skin game, making clothing and dialogue increasingly suggestive and sex scenes more graphic. Soap operas are a notable example. One father who discovered his nine-year-old daughter was watching them after school viewed a couple of episodes with her and decided it was time for a talk. "You see, Mary," he began, "this is just a story. In real life people don't usually meet someone and then immediately hop into bed with them."

"Oh, I know that," his daughter replied confidently. "They always have a drink first."[6]

Along with graphic portrayals of sex and violence, stereotyping is another of television's transgressions. Once when our daughter was a preschooler she turned from watching Saturday morning cartoons and said, "All Indians are bad aren't they, Daddy?" Although Herb assured her that there are far more good Indians than bad, he probably didn't undo the negative image she had gotten from TV.

The "scalp-hunting Indian," the "Mexican bandit," the "crotchety old man," the "buxom black mama," the "inscrutable Oriental," and the "helpless female" are stereotypes found not just in cartoons but in much of television programming.[7] Commercials are also at fault. Surely one of the more persistent stereotypes of maleness is a guy out drinking beer with his buddies; of femaleness, a woman whose most compelling concern is finding a satisfactory detergent.

Because television commercials are repeated with such frequency, their message is hammered into our conscious mind and droned into our subconscious. As many as 16 out of every 60 minutes of television programming might be taken up with commercials. By the time a child is 18 years of age, he or she will have received roughly 350,000 commercial messages totaling 5,000 viewing hours. A study done in central Minnesota showed that preschoolers actually preferred the commercials to the programs! Over half the commercials targeted specifically at children are for presweetened cereals, candy, and other sugary treats.[8]

What are the effects of television watching on children? On adults? On the national psyche? There are no conclusive answers and perhaps never will be. But for better or worse, television is definitely a part of our environment and our culture.

Setting Limits

If television is watched mindlessly and used as a mechanical child-tender, common sense tells us its influence will be negative. But when it is used with judgment and selectivity, it can, in spite of its shortcomings, be an enriching, creative force in family life. It just takes some doing to make it so.

A television set should not usurp our role as guide, teacher, and censor. Our responsibility as parents is to make rules about what may or may not be watched. There also needs to be a clear understanding about when the set can be on and for how long. How many parents would let a child go to a movie theater seven days a week and spend over three hours a day there? Few, if any. Yet that is the amount of time the average child spends watching TV.

Some families limit television viewing to one or two hours a day depending upon the age of the child. Rules concerning TV—or any rules for that matter—work best when those who will be affected by them have some input. When a time allotment is decided upon, it should be applied consistently but not inflexibly. Sometimes a worthwhile movie or special will run longer than the allotted time, and it would be unreasonable to expect a child to stop watching before it's over.

One of the advantages of limiting TV viewing time is that it encourages children to be selective about what they watch. If only one hour is permitted, who would want to waste it on just any old thing that happens to be on?

Parents who work outside the home have a difficult-to-impossible task setting limits on TV viewing. One way to gain some control over the TV situation is to help a child plan his or her day, or even an entire week. Schedule time for play, household tasks, homework, lessons, sports. Routine gives children a sense of security. It also lessens their need to switch on the TV just because they have some alone—and possibly lonely—time to fill.

We do both ourselves and our children a favor when we become acquainted with the many superb offerings on the Public Broadcasting Service. It has programs to both entertain and inform, and with far fewer commercial breaks than the commercial channels. Virtually all young children are familiar with "Sesame Street," "The Electric Company," and "Mr. Rogers," but there are many other shows on PBS—shows about nature, science, and other lands—that are engrossing to all ages.

Viewing as a Family

When parents and children view television together, it can have several positive benefits. Among them is the opportunity to help children distinguish between fantasy and reality. If a show gets scary or extremely suspenseful, it's a relief to a child to be told, "It's only a story." Although televison drama may not be real, it is realistic—so much so that it has some adults fooled. When the popular medical drama *Marcus Welby, M.D.* was on, the fictional physician received more than a quarter million letters, most seeking medical advice.[9]

Even shows that we think of as having a negative influence can have a positive benefit if we state what we feel and think without sermonizing or resorting to ridicule. We might, for instance, point out that on TV, violence is made to look like an efficient way to solve problems. What isn't shown is the pain of the person who has been injured or the emotional suffering of the dead person's survivors.

For some families, certain shows are such favorites that watching them together becomes a tradition. Maybe it's a show that causes us to laugh together or catches us up in a story line. Shared interests promote a feeling of closeness, and if that can be achieved through television, it deserves a pat on the antenna.

Often television raises questions for children. Simply watching the news with them might occasion their asking: What's civil rights? Or abortion? Or pornography? This is an opportunity to provide honest and straightforward information on topics that otherwise might not come up when we're available to discuss them.

Making a Statement with the "Off" Switch

There's an old saw that goes, "Children act like their parents no matter how hard the parents try to make them be good." With this in mind, we need to look at our own TV viewing habits. If we automatically switch the set on and demonstrate very little selectivity about what we watch, we can hardly expect our children to do otherwise. The tendency for people who can't find what they like on television is to like what they find. Perhaps that's why the major networks don't consider it necessary to deliver any higher quality programming than they already do and offer little except reruns every summer.

When a program is utterly tasteless, switching the set off is the most meaningful statement we can make. It tells children more about our standards than a whole arsenal of words. And it just might say to them that using the "off" switch is an option they can, and ought to, exercise whenever television isn't worth their time.

Expanding Possibilities

New technologies are enlarging the possibilities of what can be done with a television set. Now that cable TV is getting established, there is reason to hope that television of the future will have more diversity in programming for both children and adults. Some communities already have a local cable channel for which viewers are invited to produce their own shows and have them aired. In the city where we live, the equipment to do the filming and editing is provided by the community education center. Our fifteen-year-old son and a group of his friends learned how to use the equipment. Then they went to a miniature golf course and did a spoof of professional golf tournaments. The planning, filming, and editing were an enjoyable learning experience, and watching their creation on TV was great fun for the whole family.

For families able to afford their own videotape equipment, a lot of possibilities open up. It's easy to record everything from sporting events and school plays to birthday parties and other celebrations. Videotapes thus become the counterpart of the family picture album and in time will be cherished more than when they were made.

One mother uses a VCR to tape National Geographic shows and other programs that she feels are appropriate for her four small children. On Saturday morning she plays them instead of switching on the cartoons. "The kids are content as long as something on the screen moves," she said, "and it gets them away from all those commercials for sugar-coated cereals."

An ever-increasing number of movies for videocassette recorders can be purchased or rented. Those who bemoan that they don't "make movies like they used to" are likely to find that some of those films so fondly remembered are now on cassettes. Teens have discovered that showing a video movie at home is a good activity around which to plan a party.

Video games can get family members interacting with one another. The games range from classics like chess and checkers to simulated sporting events and arcade-type games. Yet another possibility is to connect a computer terminal to the TV and create your own video games.

TV or not TV? For most of us that is not the question. Television is so much a part of our lives that in the average household the set is on almost seven hours a day.[10] The question thus becomes, Can we make TV a creative force in family life? The answer is yes, and doing so is well worth the resolve and effort it takes.

Some Things to Try

- Keep track of your TV viewing time for a week. Make a chart on which each family member puts down the names of the shows she or he watches and the time spent. Doing so will tell a lot about each person's viewing habits and perhaps lead to an assessment of how time might be better spent.
- Write to the TV networks about shows you find praiseworthy and those you don't. According to the secretary of a major network executive, "Not one letter is thrown into the wastebasket. Just one or two letters may have a great impact on the future of any program." When writing, be calm and specific as well as brief. If you like a show, explain why. If you don't like one, explain why you find it objectionable. Encourage children to write about

shows and commercials they like and dislike. Also, suggest that they write about subjects they would enjoy seeing but are not offered. The three major networks are:
CBS
51 West 52nd Street
New York, NY 10019

NBC
30 Rockefeller Plaza
New York, NY 10020

ABC
1330 Avenue of the Americas
New York, NY 10019
- Join an organization that works for quality programming on television. Action for Children's Television (ACT) is a national nonprofit child-advocacy group working to encourage diversity in children's television and to eliminate commercial abuses targeted at children. Founded in 1968, the organization has more than 20,000 members across the country and the support of major organizations concerned with children. For more information contact:
Action for Children's Television
46 Austin Street
Newtonville, MA 02160
(617) 527-7870

You may, however, not have to look any further than your local Parent Teacher Association. This organization—which nationally has 6.5 million members—opposes TV violence and crusades for better programming. Force of numbers gives the organization considerable clout.
- Protest objectionable shows by refusing to buy the products advertised on them. Then write to both the network *and* the company whose product you are boycotting. Explain your objections and the action you have taken.
- Have a variety of games suitable for the ages of the children in the family. The games need not be expensive; checkers, cards, and dominos are three long-standing favorites. Two or three times a week, take an hour you

would otherwise spend watching television and play games with the family.

6

Discovering the Power of Prayer

Growing in the Spirit

"Can you tell me who made you?" the pastor asked a little boy.

After a moment of thoughtful consideration, the boy replied, "God made part of me."

"What do you mean, 'part of you'?"

"Well," answered the boy, "God made me little. I grew the rest myself."

"Growing the rest" is a lifetime job for all of us. Created body and soul, we are meant to grow spiritually as well as physically. One of the surest ways to develop spiritually is through prayer. "We are always in the presence of God," stated Teresa of Avila, "yet it seems to me that those who pray are in the presence in a very special sense."[1]

To pray is to talk to God. Our conversations can be as formal as praying the official prayers of our church, or as informal as the intimate outpouring of our hearts. In either case, the more faithfully we pray, the greater our spiritual growth.

At home we nurture growth in the spirit by teaching children to pray to a loving God who is always available, always ready to listen. When families pray together, children see prayer as an integral part of life. But children also need to know that they can speak to God at anytime and in anyplace: on a crowded bus or while walking alone, in the dark of night or in the light of a busy classroom. Children for whom prayer is natural and spontaneous have a headstart on developing a relationship with God that is warm and personal.

Time for Prayer

Although prayers can be said in snatched moments, God's friendship—like any other—must be nurtured and given time to grow. A teen in a religion class I once taught expressed this understanding well. "I always feel like praying when I'm very low or very happy—'God, help me' or 'Praise God' type prayers," she said. "But I'm trying to pray on a more day-to-day basis. After all, real friends don't wait for extra good or bad times to get in touch with each other."

If we want to become proficient at playing tennis or operating a computer, we have to spend hours learning how. And if we want to grow in our prayer life, we have to take time for it as well. We can read about prayer and discuss it endlessly, but unless we actually pray we'll never discover its power. "If you make a habit of sincere prayer," wrote the distinguished physician Alexis Carrel, "your life will be very noticeably and profoundly altered. Prayer is the most powerful form of energy that one can generate."[2]

Time for prayer needs to be worked into our days the way we schedule any activity that's important to us. The place we pray can be anywhere that provides quiet and privacy. The time spent in reflective prayer might be as little as five minutes or as long as we care to make it. The amount of time is not as important as praying on a regular basis.

A Maturing Prayer Life

Sometimes we pray in gratitude and praise for God's blessings. But more typically, our prayers are "me" centered. We ask God to help us on the job or in our family life or to get us through an illness. Children tend to barrage God with requests, and often ask for material goods. Although it's natural for children to pray for bikes and baseball mitts, there's a danger they'll think of God as a kind of heavenly shipping clerk and become disillusioned if they don't get what they pray for. As much as possible, children should be steered toward prayers of praise and of thanksgiving for blessings they have already received. When children do pray for things and their prayers go unanswered, we can point out that God sometimes answers by saying, "No" or "Wait awhile." As children grow older, we might suggest they pray for the ingenuity and opportunity to earn what they want.

We are maturing in our prayer life when we stop asking God to do this and that for us and ask instead for the help to help ourselves. Prayers then become requests for the courage to bear our burdens, the compassion to forgive, the wisdom to understand. Eleanor Roosevelt didn't wait around for God to do what she saw needed doing. But she didn't just rely on her own and other human resources either. Following is a prayer she always carried in her purse: "Our Father, who has set a restlessness in our hearts and made us all seekers after that which we can never fully find, . . . keep us at tasks too hard for us, that we may be driven to Thee for strength."[3]

Ask and You Shall Receive

Scripture tells us, "Whatever you ask in prayer, believe that you have received it, and it will be yours" (Mark 11:24, RSV). That claim sounds too good to be true, but those who put it to the test know it has validity. And many who have had their prayers answered add a cautionary note: Be careful what you pray for, because once you get it, you might not want it!

One praying technique is to see ourselves as already having what we are praying for. The practice is popularly called "imaging," but the basis is scriptural. In the above passage from Mark, the operative words are "believe that you have received it."

To illustrate, let's say that a student is praying to pass a difficult exam. In her mind's eye, she sees herself taking the test and knowing the answers. Maybe she even visualizes how happy she is when the grades are posted and others are congratulating her. Although imaging may sound like daydreaming, it is more. Much more. Creating the image is just the beginning. This young woman does not stop studying; she simply studies with a positive attitude and believes she is going to do well on the test. Holding fast to the image becomes an expression of faith that is nurtured by prayer.

Imaging is practiced by many of the world's great achievers. Some no doubt do it instinctively. Jim Thorpe, one of this country's finest athletes, is known to have put imaging to work for himself. Once on a ship that was carrying him to the Olympics, many stars were running around the deck or doing other rigorous exercise. When the coach spotted his decathlon entrant sitting with his eyes closed, he demanded to know what he was doing.

"Just practicing," Thorpe replied, then explained that while relaxing he was seeing himself competing successfully in his specialty. Jim Thorpe's triumphs and record-breaking performances in the 1912 Olympics are part of history.[4] This is not to suggest that he gave up training in favor of imaging, only that the two things working together helped make him great.

In the 1984 Olympics, gymnast Mary Lou Retton also used imaging to her advantage. Before going to sleep at night, it was her custom to image her performances. "I see myself hitting all my routines, doing everything perfectly," the sixteen-year-old athlete told a reporter. "I imagine all the moves and go through them with the image in my mind."[5] In the final event, her performance earned her a perfect ten and a gold medal.

Prayer isn't a requisite for imaging. But when prayer is combined with images that are compatible with God's will for us, amazing things can happen. An exciting adventure in prayer awaits anyone who tries it. When I introduced the concept to our daughter, she was eager to begin. Today, many months later, she remains enthusiastic about its benefits. Old and young alike are sometimes lukewarm about prayer only because they have never explored its potential and possibilities.

What Is God Saying to Me?

Prayer involves listening as well as talking. But how is God going to get in touch with us? Are we going to hear voices or see a message written in the sky? Such possibilities are remote. Peter Marshall, once a well-known chaplain in the United States Senate, felt that generally God speaks to us through our own conscience—we get a growing conviction that such and such a course of action is the one to take. At times, God speaks through our families or friends or others who provide sound judgment. There are also those times when God speaks through our own circumstances, closing one door and opening another.[6]

Author Ardis Whitman tells of an experience in which she talked to God in prayer, listened, and found her answer.

Having missed a train, Mrs. Whitman was stranded in a strange city with time on her hands and in no mood to enjoy herself. There had been a quarrel in her family the day before, and she was still troubled by it. Looking back at the incident, she wrote:

> Finally, I strayed in through the open door of a church and sat quietly for a while, not so much praying as talking to God. "I did everything I could," I protested. "It wasn't my fault." Silence. Then I felt a compelling urge to look again, think again; an urge to go back to a certain day, a certain hour. As on a screen, I saw that hour unroll. I saw the interplay of the characters as though I were not involved; and suddenly I saw—peacefully, without anguish—a new version of my role and my family's, a new way to bring us together.

Walking out into the sunlight, I thought in wonderment, "God spoke to me," though in fact, I had heard no words.[7]

Pray for One Another

The same power of prayer that can so dramatically affect our own lives can also be used to affect the lives of others. General James L. Dozier, who was kidnapped and held captive by an Italian terrorist organization, is convinced that it was prayer—his and the prayers of others—that brought him through the ordeal. Recounting his forty-two days in captivity, General Dozier wrote:

> In spite of my predicament . . . I am helped by something quite strong, a force supporting me like the lift one feels from an ocean wave, a powerful buoyancy . . . . A vivid impression came to me of my executive officer. He is a deep-thinking friend. I've always felt confident about bouncing my thoughts off him. At first I wondered why I felt his presence so closely; then I knew. He was praying for me. I felt invigorated.
>
> A few days later . . . I sensed the closeness of another friend. He teaches in the American school in Verona and is a gentle man who truly lives by his faith.
>
> It happened again. . . . This time it was an American missionary who ministers to American servicemen . . . . I know he is ministering to me.

After General Dozier was safely rescued, he compared notes with the officer, the schoolteacher, and the missionary. He discovered that at the times when he strongly sensed the closeness of these friends, they were earnestly praying for him. In view of his experience, General Dozier maintains, ". . . our prayers for others, expressed in the love of God, can be our most powerful communication with them, transcending time and space."[8]

Scripture tells us to "pray for one another" (James 5:16, RSV). As General Dozier's experience indicates, it is one of the most generous and helpful ways we have of ministering to others. And it can be done by anyone, anywhere, anytime.

Ask and It Shall Be Given

There are a lot of references to prayer in Scripture, and some of the claims about it are bold indeed. Surely one of the boldest claims is, "Ask, and it will be given you; seek, and you will find; knock, and it will be opened to you. For every one who asks receives, and he who seeks finds, and to him who knocks it will be opened" (Matthew 7:7-11, RSV). Yet anyone who has ever prayed has had prayers go unanswered. Or so it seems. Even Jesus did not receive everything he asked for. While in the garden of Gethsemane, he asked to be relieved of his cross, praying, "take this cup of suffering from me" (Luke 22:42, TEV). But the crucifixion proceeded. This wasn't the answer Jesus asked for, but it was part of a larger picture, for it led to the resurrection and Jesus' victory over death. Likewise, the answers we receive are sometimes wiser than our prayers. This idea is made clear in a prayer believed to have been written during the Civil War by a Confederate soldier.

> I asked God for strength, that I might achieve;
> I was made weak, that I might learn humbly to obey.
> I asked for health, that I might do greater things;
> I was given infirmity that I might do better things.
> I asked for riches, that I might be happy;
> I was given poverty, that I might be wise.
> I asked for power, that I might have the praise of men;
> I was given weakness, that I might feel the need of God.
> I asked for all things, that I might enjoy life;
> I was given life, that I might enjoy all things.
> I got nothing that I asked for—but everything I had hoped for.

Almost despite myself, my unspoken prayers were answered.

I am, among all men, most richly blessed.

Living Prayer

Not all prayers are put into words. The spirit with which we live and the way we treat others in God's name are prayers too. Prayer can become a way of life. Or, looked at another way, life properly lived is a way of prayer. "More things are wrought by prayer than this world dreams of," wrote the poet Tennyson.[9] It is a truth each of us can discover for ourselves. All we need do is make prayer an earnest and indispensable part of our lives. Peace and strength will then come to us, and through us.

Some Things to Try

- Make bedtime for young children a time of peacefulness and prayer. Encourage spontaneous prayers in which your child simply talks to God about his or her day. To begin, pray aloud yourself so your child realizes that we can talk to God the way we talk to a friend.
- When children pray, listen to see if they show awareness of others and their needs; if they thank God for the blessings in life; if they seek forgiveness; if there is a desire to be better. When children's prayers seem self-centered, gently suggest the names of people they might pray for and the blessings for which they might give thanks.
- Develop the habit of mealtime prayer in your family in a way that seems right and natural for you. You may want to pray a formal grace, speak your own made-up prayers, read from the Bible, sing songs that praise God and creation, or recite a poem. Candles help create a reverent atmosphere and make praying at meals special. If making up your own prayers seems stiff and unnatural, start by saying a memorized grace, and invite each member of the family to add something personal.

- Join a prayer group. Amazing things happen when a number of people focus the power of their prayers for a single purpose. Also, one can find much spiritual nurturing and support in such a group.
- Post prayers where they will be seen frequently by everyone in the family. Two of the most likely places are the bathroom mirror and the refrigerator door. Compose a prayer, or use one that has already been written. Ask family members to take turns posting a prayer.
- Express one of your prayers in the form of a letter. Remember that God is a friend, so write about anything on your mind—what's troubling you, what you're thankful for, what you need and want. Anything at all. When you've finished, seal the letter in an envelope and put it away for a few weeks or months. Then look at the letter and see what has happened since you wrote it. Putting hopes down on paper is a form of imaging. When the workings of the subconscious are combined with prayers, goals have an uncanny way of becoming reality. Writing prayer letters might be a family activity. Although the letters are not shared, the changes that occur in the lives of the family members can be.
- Read some of the many good books available on prayer. One book that simply and effectively helps the reader follow the scriptural directive to "pray constantly" (1 Thessalonians 5:17, RSV) is *The Breath of Life: Discovering Your Breath Prayer*, by Ron DelBene with Herb Montgomery (Winston Press).

7

Growing into a Faith

Faith Begins at Home

An idealized picture of family living shows parents and children happily going off to church together. They appear to be the epitome of right living, and well they might be. But worshipping as a family is only the frosting on the cake. The real substance of religion happens, or fails to happen, at home. The question is, How do we make home a place where faith takes root? What can we do to foster the values and attitudes that we profess to believe when we come together to worship?

Children's earliest feelings about religion are closely linked to what we, their parents, say and do. When children are young, they get their sense of security from us and imitate our behavior and attitudes. If we are caring and honest, that is the way they will tend to be. If we are reverent believers, they will believe simply because we do. The Reverend John E. Corrigan in his writings on moral development states:

> The surer the child matures as a person in a religious home, the more certain he is to be religious as an adult. . . . children will develop their own practices based on values they have discerned. The essential, at least for the parents, is to give the children the standards by which to form and measure their values.[1]

Does God Have a Car?

If we believe there is a God and say so, young children give us no arguments. But they will have questions. They may want to know: Can I see God? Does God have a car? Does God like me? Although some children's questions about God may seem silly to us, they are serious to the child and deserve the best answer we can give. It's tempting to give more information than children want to know or can absorb, but remember that children process information at their own speed. When they are ready for more they will ask.

What is the picture of God that we want our children to have? Do we want them to believe in a God who is caring and forgiving? Or do we want them to think of God as rigid and judgmental, more to be feared than loved? The God we introduce children to will tend to be the one that was presented to us. But we *can* discard old concepts and adopt new ones.

In my own childhood, God was presented as stern and demanding. I pictured him as a kind of grouchy grandfather in the sky, and I was sure he was always waiting to catch me doing something wrong. This kept me walking a pretty straight line, but it is not the view of God I have since adopted, and certainly not the one I wanted for my children. I hoped they would view God as loving and approachable, someone who would understand and forgive. Thus Herb and I always talked about God in that context, believing that children are more apt to grow close to someone they love than someone they fear.

"Particularly in the age period from three to six, the child's readiness to love and depend on God, or to fear God, develops," notes the venerable Doctor Spock.[2] Because young children have such active imaginations, he cautions against ever talking about God's wrath or hellfire, fearing that the pictures they conjure up will be much too terrifying.

On the other hand, recent studies show that introducing children to a God of love has many benefits. Young people who learn about a compassionate God tend to be more active in extracurricular activities and have fewer problems with authorities. Also, they are more likely to do better in school and start sexual activity later than children who are taught that God is austere and vengeful.[3]

Children in Church

Including young children in our Sunday worship is a nice idea, but often it isn't the uplifting experience we hope it will be. It can, in fact, be the biggest hassle of the week. Too often, parents who bring their children to church spend much of their time riveting the kids with disapproving looks, whispering warnings, squeezing an arm, or using some equally harsh means of physical control.

Young children are usually not at their best in church. And how can we expect them to be? Often they have to sit where they see only backs and elbows, and yet they are supposed to be attentive to a worship service that has no meaning for them. Early in our parenting we considered options such as leaving the children at home, sitting apart with them in the "crying room," or using the church's nursery. Usually we opted to worship as a family and found ways to make it rewarding for all of us.

Let Children Be Children

Children need to be children. That doesn't mean they should be noisy and disruptive. What it means is that asking a preschooler to sit at full attention for an hour or more is asking too much. When our children were this age, church meant a lot of lap-sitting time, which they loved. During a busy week, parents often don't get the chance to hold a child as much as they, or the child, would like. Sitting in church enfolded in the warm circle of a parent's arms is one of the surest ways of helping a child sense the love of God.

Another strategy for keeping children content in church is to bring along something with which they can quietly amuse themselves. We had a selection of books set aside just as "church books." That is not to say they were all expressly religious, only that they were books the children looked at while in church. To keep interest high, we added new books from time to time.

When one of our children was a preschooler, he especially liked to draw. So along with the church books we always brought drawing paper and watercolor markers. During those years, he had a particular fondness for trains. Using the pew seat for a drawing board, he quietly churned out trains on Sunday mornings. These we admiringly referred to as "church art." In his own time, he drew less and less and sat listening more and more.

As children get older, we naturally expect them to sit still longer and be more attentive. They don't have to understand everything that's going on at a worship service to get some benefit from it. Just being together with the family in an activity that the parents value can be reason enough to be present. But if children are going to value Sunday worship, they have to make sense out of it. What can we do to instill an appreciation for ritual and liturgy? For a starter, we can arrive at church early enough to get a seat where our child can see what's going on. Through classroom instruction or our own explanations, children can be taught the various parts of the service. Also, worship services can be geared to young people; when that occurs, they are likely to be meaningful. A priest friend relates that when he was growing up, there was a 9:15 Mass just for kids. He loved it because the priest always talked about a creature from another planet who was interested in the Catholic religion.

When They Don't Want to Go to Church

No matter what we do to give meaning and importance to Sunday worship, there may come a time when our children don't want to go with us. This occurs most commonly in the teen years, but one of our children didn't wait that long. He was about nine when his I'm-only-going-because-you're-making-me attitude got very wearying. Much to his surprise, we agreed to let him stay home one Sunday. But there were conditions. He was not to watch television. He could, however, read a book, listen to music, or do something with paints and crayons. And by the time we got home, he was to have filled in the ten blanks on a sheet of paper with the heading THESE ARE THINGS I THANK GOD FOR. When we came home, one of the things he had listed being thankful for was "relijun." The next Sunday, and for many Sundays after that, we heard no more complaints about going to church.

Another approach to children who don't want to go to church is to liken church attendance to going to school. Suppose they became bored with school; would we let them drop out? Even if by law they were old enough to quit, we'd be shunning our responsibility if we said, "Okay, if that's how you feel, go ahead and do it." We know they need an education and that the older they get, the more they will think so, too.

We can explain that we feel much the same way about church attendance. It's something they need. If they didn't go, they wouldn't take the time to worship God. As they get older we can hope they will see the value of going to church, but in the meantime we let them know that it's our job to keep them involved.[4]

As daughters and sons move into the teen years, they search for their own identities. They want to do things their way, not ours. Some families find that teenagers are more willing to attend church if they can choose which service to go to and to sometimes go by themselves. As one fifteen-year-old boy explained, "Mass has a different effect on me when I go by myself. When you're with your family, you sort of blend into the group. When I'm there alone, I feel as if the priest is talking to *me*."[5]

Attending to Our Own Faith

In the teen years, young people seek answers to the insistent questions, *Who am I? Why am I here? What is the meaning of life?* These are questions to which all religions address themselves, but church attendance may not be helping a particular son or daughter find answers. After we've used up all our persuasions about why they should go, and they're still intent upon rejecting their religion (and perhaps all religions), what do we do? Do we take a hard line and rant, "As long as you're a member of this family and live in this house, you're going to church with us"? Or do we try to be understanding and empathetic, realizing that their feelings about attending church might be similar to the way we feel about attending a soccer game or a symphony? If we take the hard line and insist on church attendance, the battle lines are drawn and the worship service becomes a weapon rather than a prayer. We can force young people to kneel, stand, and sit, but we cannot force them to believe or to pray.

When a teen's ideas about religion differ from ours, it's tempting to cut them off, to simply not listen. Yet this is contrary to the religion we profess to believe. Jesus said, "Do for others what you want them to do for you . . ." (Matthew 7:12, TEV). That means speaking to our children the way we want them to speak to us. It means being courteous and respectful of their opinions even though they may differ radically from our own. And it means admitting that we don't have all the answers.

Once we have admitted we are not all-knowing, it might start us attending to our own faith—really attending to it. Just going to church doesn't make us practicing Christians. Practicing our faith implies living it daily. And growing in faith has to do with learning more about why we believe as we do. Although it may seem rash, we might at least consider telling our questioning teenagers they can skip church for a while if they are willing to learn more about their religion. This may mean that you have to find information, digest it, and set aside a time when you and your teenager discuss spirituality in general and your family's religion in particular. The time for this might be after you have returned from church on Sunday, or after the main meal that day. Remember, this should be a time to share, not to lecture. Lecturing antagonizes. Sharing fosters closeness and good will.

Religion Needs to Fit

If our children reject the faith we had trusted they would carry on, it can mean great disappointment and much heartache for us. But it is no reason to despair. We are all on a spiritual journey, and each of us must find our own way. After all, do we really want our children to accept a hand-me-down religion without determining if it fits them? I don't believe so. Children should be taught not just to answer questions, but to question answers. When they have taken the religion we are passing on to them, have doubted and probed and ended up accepting it as their own, we have real cause for rejoicing. Then worshipping together means that our family is truly united in faith by choice, not by chance or by pressure.

Some Things to Try

- Make Sundays special. Depending upon the time you attend church, go out for breakfast or lunch occasionally. After church, plan to visit friends, or invite friends from church to your house.
- Take part in an after-church fellowship. If beverages and snacks are not already being served in your church after at least one of the services, consider organizing something that will get parishioners mingling socially after worshipping together.
- From time to time, attend services in a church other than the one to which you belong. Going someplace different enlivens children's interest. For adults it often provides new insights and perspectives about worship and prevailing attitudes toward religion.
- Join a Bible-study group or take a class that provides an opportunity to know more about your religion.

- If your church has a liturgy committee, investigate the possibility of joining.
- Consider whether the parish you currently belong to is really your church home. Some parishes are conservative in nature, some liberal, and still others somewhere in between. Families who have a liberal orientation can feel out of place in a conservative parish and vice versa. You will be a much happier and more productive member of the church community if you and your family have a strong sense of belonging that is based on shared attitudes concerning your faith.

8

Forgiving and Forgetting

How Difficult It Is!

The feud between the Hatfields and McCoys is part of American folk history. Begun in the nineteenth century in the mountains of West Virginia, the fighting took thirty to fifty lives over a period of thirty years. Even though the bloodshed stopped, it wasn't until 1976 that the two patriarchs in the families shook hands and ended America's most famous misunderstanding. The cause of the feud? It remains unknown.[1]

The case of the Hatfields and McCoys is extreme, but even in the ordinary circumstances in our lives, it's often easier to continue old animosities than to set them right. Virtually all of us have difficulties with forgiveness: difficulties with forgiving others, with asking for forgiveness, accepting it when it is offered, and especially with forgiving ourselves. "Everyone thinks forgiveness is a lovely idea," wrote noted author C. S. Lewis, "until they have something to forgive."[2]

Difficult as forgiveness may be, it is the bone-deep essence of our Christian faith. In the prayer Jesus taught, he said, "forgive us our trespasses as we forgive those who trespass against us." And in another part of the Gospels we are told, "If you are bringing your offering to the altar, and there remember that your brother has something against you, leave your gift there before the altar and go; first be reconciled to your brother, and then come back and offer your gift" (Matthew 5:23-24, RSV). Jesus himself was the ultimate reconciler. He died forgiving his killers, living out what he had been teaching all along.

The Urge to Get Even

Our human reaction to injury is to retaliate, to hurt our enemy as we have been hurt. But Jesus came to convince us that evil can be overcome with goodness. His words and his actions carried the message that we must break the cycle of an "eye for an eye" and a "tooth for a tooth." By hurting an enemy we perpetuate evil; by forgiving we promote goodness.

We frequently find, however, that the values of our religion are inconsistent with the message we get from society. Grudge-bearing skills are applauded. "Don't get mad, get even" is a philosophy that's widely approved. When put to use in our daily lives, getting even makes us look strong, look like people who aren't going to be pushed around. Practiced in the extreme, the result is terrorism. When yet another embassy is attacked or yet another bomb is set off in a crowded department store, the media state that a certain terrorist organization "claims responsibility" or "takes credit." Apparently it is something in which the terrorists take pride. They have gotten even. But getting even only worsens the situation. Whether in personal relationships or social issues, there has to be forgiveness before positive change can come about. Failure to forgive makes us prisoners of old grievances and prevents us from getting on with new business. Not the least, failing to forgive creates stresses that lead to physical illness.

A conservative estimate among doctors is that emotional turmoil brings on at least fifty percent of the ailments they see in patients—ailments such as ulcers, heart trouble, rashes, high blood pressure. One physician tells of a man who had nurtured a long-time hatred of another person and actually died of "grudgitis." Although it was not entered as the official cause of death, the doctor related how the patient's color turned ashen and his eyes lost their luster. His whole being deteriorated, leaving his organs lacking in resistance and vulnerable to disease.[3]

Amazing Things Can Happen

The fullness of health is achieved when mind, body, and spirit are in harmony. That kind of well-being can only come about if the burdens of guilt and resentment are dropped. A thirty-two-year-old real estate broker who wanted inner healing went to great lengths seeking forgiveness. Traveling to a city halfway across the country, he contacted the man whose apartment he had burglarized fourteen years earlier. Handing the victim a $50 bill, a $20 bill, and a $5 bill, he said, "I feel like this makes restitution." The one-time burglar blamed his criminal behavior on heavy drinking and said that he now wanted to make it up "to all the people he had experienced problems with."[4] In another case, a Florida stockbroker took out a newspaper ad to express his apology for a wrong he had committed forty-six years earlier. "Viola, I am sorry," read the ad in which the man confessed to wrongly naming a six-year-old classmate as the thief of a penny's worth of peanut butter and crackers in 1938.[5]

There are people for whom granting forgiveness is a way to bring some good out of a tragic situation. When a drunken driver killed their twenty-three-year-old son, the parents requested that the driver perform community service instead of being sent to prison. The judge obliged, and the offender was ordered to work 1,500 hours as a nursing assistant in a trauma center where the state's severest accident cases are treated. The dead son was one of eight children, and the parents said that by their action they wanted to instill in their other children the Christian ethic of forgiveness.[6]

The way these parents reacted runs contrary to the way most of us tend to behave when we have been wronged. Whether in large matters or small, our whole being tends to scream out against forgiving the offender. We feel we have a right to our resentment and our anger. But when we free ourselves of them, we have a new zest for living that compels us to leave yesterday behind and get on with today.

Let Forgiveness Begin at Home

When forgiveness is practiced at home, a family can overcome everything from petty misunderstandings to major conflicts. Forgiveness makes the difference between an angry, spite-filled house and a happy place where everyday hurts and annoyances are pardoned and laid to rest. Practicing understanding and forbearance in small matters is good preparation for forgiving more significant injuries and blunders. To whatever degree we love and forgive, we live out the call of the gospel message.

Jesus used parables to teach us how all-forgiving God is. One such parable describes a loving father who joyously welcomed home his errant son. Another parable portrays a shepherd who leaves his flock to search for one lost sheep. If our children are to comprehend such a caring, forgiving God, they need to have the experience of being forgiven by at least one person whose love for them is unconditional. They need a parent who lets them know that although they do bad things, they are not bad people, that they can be forgiven and make a new beginning. How do we accomplish this? The first and most obvious way is simply to say, "I forgive you." We must, however, *mean* the words when we say them. I recall once telling my son I had forgiven him only to have him look at me dejectedly and say, "But your eyes are still mad at me!"

One way to reassure our children—or for that matter, anyone—that our words of forgiveness are sincere is to accompany them with a hug, a squeeze of the hand, a smile. Once we have forgiven someone, we need to make a new beginning. That may mean biting the tongue to keep from bringing the matter up again. "I can forgive, but I can't forget" is only another way of saying, "I won't forgive."

A Way to Be Healed and Free

Forgiveness heals relationships and frees the spirit. The one who forgives is freed of resentment, and the one who has been forgiven is free to grow and to love. That makes forgiveness sound easy, maybe even a bit sentimental. Well, forgiveness is neither. It is difficult. And there are no formulas or easy answers to make it less so. But there are some suggestions and guidelines to help answer the questions that forgiveness inevitably raises.

"How can I possibly forgive that?"

Consider the alternative. Holding onto a grudge will only make the hurt deepen and harden until it becomes a destructive force in our lives. We need first to look squarely at the injury and acknowledge our hurt and anger. Then begins the work of finding a way to forgive. The great statesman Benjamin Disraeli is said to have put the name of anyone who injured him on a slip of paper and locked it up in a drawer. This action was like an eraser that put the matter out of his mind.

Inspirational author Catherine Marshall wrote about acting literally on Jesus' words, "When you stand to pray, forgive anything you may have against anyone . . ." (Mark 11:25, TEV). She and her husband put on paper any grievances they held against anybody. Then they read them aloud, forgave the persons involved, and destroyed the papers.[7]

Scripture tells us "If you forgive others the wrongs they have done to you, your Father in heaven will also forgive you. But if you do not forgive others, then your Father will not forgive the wrongs you have done" (Matthew 6:14-15, TEV). In other words, we must find a way to forgive because refusing to do so breaks the bridge over which we ourselves are to pass.

"What if I don't feel like forgiving?"

Our feelings need not control us; we can control them. To forgive or not to forgive is our choice. If we cannot find it in our heart to forgive, we can pray for the strength to do it.

The very act of spilling out our annoyances and injuries in prayer takes some of the sting out of them and makes us better able to view them objectively. Beyond prayer, some action is called for. It might be a letter we write, a kindness we perform, a hug, a heartfelt "I'm sorry" either face to face or over the phone.

In a startling drama of forgiveness and reconciliation, Pope John Paul II went to the cell where his would-be assassin was imprisoned. Taking the hand that had held the gun meant to kill him, the Pope forgave Mehmet Ali Agca. Commenting on the meeting, an Italian writer stated, "The Pope intends to say, 'If we really want peace, we must make the first step, we must forget offenses and offer the bread of love and charity.'"[8]

If we choose to forgive, we too will have chosen to love.

"How could he (she) do that to me?"

There's an old French saying that goes "To understand all is to forgive all." When we have been wronged, we need first to consider whether the injury might have been unintentional or unavoidable. The next consideration is what pressures the person may have been under: poor health, family problems, job insecurity, financial worries. We are generally willing to forgive to the extent that we can see the other's point of view or reason for the action.

It is also well to remember that none of us is without fault. We all fall short of being the people God calls us to be. But ours is the God of forgiveness, the God of the second chance. As Christ-followers we are called to pass the gift of forgiveness on to others.

"How can I forgive again?"

When Peter asked if forgiving an offender seven times was enough—thinking no doubt he would be praised for his largesse—he was told no, it must be "seventy times seven" (Matthew 18:22, RSV). In other words, forgiveness is a mere token unless it is unlimited.

Human as we are, that seems too much to ask. But our capacity for forgiveness enlarges when we stop trying to fit people to our mold of what we think they should be and start accepting them as they are. Relationships can deepen if we're willing to suspend judgments and accept people who fall short of our expectations. It then becomes easier to forgive a child for being reckless or a friend for always being late. Although forgiving "seventy times seven" will never be easy, it does become a possibility.

"Can I forgive people but not like them?"

God never said that if someone strikes us on the left cheek, we should kiss the attacker on the right. Or if we walk the second mile in an attempt to be reconciled, the finale does not call for a warm embrace. The essence of forgiveness is to love our enemies out of consideration for God, whose child that enemy happens to be. When we think of ourselves as children of God—brothers and sisters, each with our own particular strengths and shortcomings—forgiveness becomes easier.

"How can I forgive myself?"

When we're down on ourselves over some wrong we've committed, it's well to look at those things we've done right. It puts matters in perspective and we see our misstep as part of the larger fabric of life. Once we've made amends to God and anyone we may have harmed, we need to put the incident behind us—to forgive our own trespasses as we forgive those of others. "It takes charity to forgive someone else," states a Greek adage; "it takes wisdom to forgive yourself."

Some Things to Try

- When you make a mistake in dealing with a child, apologize. If you can't bring yourself to do so immediately, do it when the time seems opportune. An honest apology has a way of making parent and child feel particularly close.
- Pray for anyone who injures you by word or deed. It's hard to stay angry with someone you pray for.

- A lot of small family grievances can be dispatched with a light touch. After one father had lectured his son at length, the son said, "Nobody's perfect," and with a sly grin added, "except you." The point was made, and they both laughed.
- Get a piece of paper and write down the names of those against whom you feel resentful or have held a longtime grudge. Alongside the name write the offense and why you think the person acted as he or she did. Ask God to help lift your burden of resentment. Then destroy the paper. This activity might be part of the suggested family reconciliation service that follows.
- Hold a family reconciliation service at home. It can take as little as ten minutes after the evening meal. (Full stomachs generally make people more agreeable and ready to try something new.) Lighted candles and appropriate music help create a reverent atmosphere. Open with a prayer. You may want to hold hands and say the Lord's Prayer or use a prayer such as

  > We gather today, God, to consider our relationships with one another. Help us be more open in our communication and more sensitive to the needs of others. Guide us in finding ways to make our home a place of honesty, compassion, and love. We ask this in the name of Jesus, who taught us how to love and how to forgive. Amen.

- Read the story of the Prodigal Son (Luke 15:11-32). Discuss the different characters in the story—father, wayward son, servants, oldest son, farmer who gave the boy a job, friends who stayed behind. Ask which of the characters family members most identify with. Why? Responses can reveal a lot about family relationships—where they are strained and where they are strong. Ask everyone to share a way in which he or she can contribute to making the family function more harmoniously. (For example, get up earlier so there is less chaos in the morning; ask before borrowing; refrain from monopolizing the telephone.)

  Close with the prayer of St. Francis:

Lord, make me an instrument of your peace;
where there is hatred, let me sow love;
where there is injury, pardon;
where there is doubt, faith;
where there is despair, hope;
where there is darkness, light;
where there is sadness, joy.
Oh divine master,
grant that I may not so much seek to be consoled
    as to console;
to be understood, as to understand;
to be loved, as to love.
For it is in giving that we receive;
it is in pardoning that we are pardoned;
and it is in dying that we are born to eternal life.

9

Keeping Christ in Christmas

Where's Jesus?

Plans for the church Christmas pageant began in early December. First there were the decisions about who would be Mary and Joseph and the rest of the Christmas story's cast of characters. Then the children gathered props, and parents helped create costumes. A blue bathrobe and a white shawl seemed just right for Mary. For Joseph, there was a coarse woolen poncho that smelled of mothballs. The shepherds fashioned crooks from heavy cardboard, and the Wisemen disguised their choir robes with fur pieces scavenged from a musty attic.

When the night of the pageant arrived, the excitement rivaled opening night on Broadway. Right down to the real straw scattered about the manger, there seemed to be no detail that had been overlooked. No detail, that is, until one of the shepherds checked the manger scene and asked, "Where's Jesus?"

Indeed, where was Jesus? The cradle was in place, but it was empty. In the flurry of preparation and planning, Jesus had been overlooked.

The story makes us pause and reflect. Amid all the shopping and partying and card-sending, do we forget what Christmas is really about? Do we too overlook Jesus?

Keeping the True Spirit

There's a fanciful quality to the story of Jesus' birth. It happened under curious circumstances in a long-ago time and faraway place. Despite its seeming remoteness, the story is as relevant today as it was when it occurred. It is a story that rekindles hope, a story that reminds us anew of the mighty caring of God.

Children come to a knowledge of Jesus slowly. When they are young, they cannot comprehend Jesus as the light of the world. But being told that he is the Son of God fits into their frame of reference. They can understand that as a baby he was received with love by his earthly parents and welcomed with joy by those believers who had waited so long for his coming. When we emphasize that Christmas is the celebration of Jesus' birth, children sense that there is something infinitely special about this child who grew to be a man like, yet different from, all others. As children grow older, we want them to understand that even though we fall short of being our best, Jesus came to tell us that God never gives up on us. That is cause to rejoice and a reason to make Christmas a very special holiday.

Finding a place for Christ in Christmas doesn't mean that we have to give up the festiveness of the season. Nor does it mean that we should forgo gift giving. After all, what is more Christian than joy? And what is more spiritual than giving? Keeping the true spirit of the season alive requires only that we not get so busy with preparations and parties that, like the shepherd in the pageant, we discover that we've overlooked Jesus.

Some families make a very real effort to keep Christmas from being a time of over-wanting and over-buying. They manage to slow the season down and make it a time of shared love and joy. The inner feeling of warmth that they experience lingers long after the last of the turkey has been eaten and the decorations packed away.

One such family has a simple Advent ceremony following their Sunday night meals. With Christmas music playing softly in the background, they light the appropriate candle(s) on the Advent wreath. Next they open the week's Christmas cards and talk about the people who sent them. They also exchange thoughts about what Advent means to them and together keep finding new meaning in the season. To end their time together, one of the parents reads a Christmas story that holds the interest of their kindergartner and two preschoolers. The children's father explains, "If you don't do this kind of special planning, you proceed with the normal course of things—doing Christmas shopping in lines ten deep, watching television, or working on Christmas cards. We've found that there are more meaningful things to do."

Another family tries to remain true to the spirit of the season by inviting people who have no family to be their guests. These parents and their thirteen-year-old son and eight-year-old daughter have unofficially adopted a retarded adult friend who shares their Christmas dinner and then spends the night with them. This family also gets names of shut-ins from their church and makes visits, bringing with them home-baked goodies and other food. Along with their efforts to emphasize the essential spirit of the holidays, the family has tried to de-emphasize gift giving. The parents admit this is difficult when the children complain that their friends are getting all the latest toys being hyped on TV. "What we're trying to convey to them is that maybe we can give of ourselves," their mother said. "I hope what they get from the way we celebrate is an increased realization of what money won't buy."

A young family with one preschool child has a birthday cake for their Christmas dinner dessert. It's their way of noting that Christmas is a celebration of the birth of Jesus. The tradition is one that the mother brought to the marriage from her family.

For some families, getting at the season's real meaning comes from reading the Christmas story in Scripture (Luke 2:1-20). Others find meaning in various kinds of readings. One family with young children takes particular delight from the classic story *The Littlest Angel*. In the story, the most humble, caring gift God receives turns out to be the most special. In a family that includes teenagers, each person chooses something that is personally meaningful and reads it aloud. Through such sharing, members of this family feel they get to know one another better.

What Did You Get for Christmas?

Retailers expect to do approximately one-fourth of their yearly business during the holiday season. Typically, people admit to spending too much on gifts, or are nagged by guilt because they can't spend more. Packages piled high under Christmas trees speak both of greed and generosity. "What did you get for Christmas?" is a question put to virtually all children. It's most frequently asked by those who get a lot.

A Midwestern newspaper columnist wrote about a Christmas during the Depression when his parents had very little money. That year he received only one present: a small truck that cost eighty-nine cents. "I was thrilled," he recalled, "because I didn't know it wasn't expensive."

On Christmas Day a playmate down the block asked him what he got. With considerable pride, he told her.

"Is that all?" she asked, promptly launching into a long recitation of what she'd received.

The columnist recalls being envious and, when he got home, told his mother what the little girl had said. His mother wasn't the most educated of women, but young as the boy was, he recognized that she had her own kind of wisdom. Nestling him in her lap, she said, "You got all we could give you. I'll bet that little girl's parents could have given her even more than she got."[1]

Although many families try to cut down on lavish gift giving, they frequently find that change comes slowly. One family still gives presents, but the mother said, "We're placing more emphasis on the giving of our time and ourselves, giving rides to strangers caught walking on a snowy day, offering help to others when it's unexpected." In selecting presents for the children, she does so with an eye to what will promote sharing and cooperation—gifts such as a tape recorder and tapes, watercolor markers, books, and board games.

Some families find much pleasure in making their own gifts. It takes planning and time, but a mother who makes most of her gifts says it also takes time to find the perfect sweater for somebody or a toy for the child who has everything. If you want to make your own gifts, it's helpful to be able to cook and sew, but many gifts don't require those skills. Coupons on which the giver promises to do something for another person can be given. Any number of craft items from pencil holders to handmade birdhouses make good presents. The mother of a family that creates its gifts says they've found it a way to have a simple, gracious Christmas, one that's people-centered and spiritual.

When children receive a lot of gifts at one time, the tendency is to quickly rip the wrappings off one package so as to get on to the next . . . and the next. When we saw this happening in our young family, we tried a new approach. Starting the week before Christmas, we let the children each choose a present a day from under the tree. This they would shake, speculate as to its contents, and finally open. We discovered that gifts opened in this way were savored and appreciated much more than if they had been hurriedly opened all at once on Christmas Eve.

Another mother uses a variation of the same idea. Instead of opening a gift a day, her two children open them all on December 23rd. She feels this allows them to relish opening the gifts and to focus on the spiritual significance of Christmas Eve and Christmas Day.

Gifts for All Seasons

With a touch of creativity we can keep Christ in Christmas. But how much better if we could keep Christ in all the days of our year! Benjamin Franklin left us some suggestions regarding the gifts to give. Practiced faithfully, Franklin's ideas can keep the spirit of Christmas alive and help us grow in God's love.

The Best Things to Give
. . . to your enemy, forgiveness;
. . . to an opponent, tolerance;
. . . to a friend, your ear;
. . . to your child, good example;
. . . to parents, conduct that will make them proud of you;
. . . to yourself, respect;
. . . to all, charity.

Some Things to Try

- Start or continue the tradition of lighting Advent-wreath candles. Purchase a wreath or make one at home. All you need is a circle of greenery in which to place four candles—three purple and one pink. The purple candles symbolize our need to be forgiven, and the pink one is a reminder that Advent is a time of joyful expectation. Some people stand a fifth candle (white) in the center of the wreath. This "Christ candle" is lit on Christmas Eve. Placing the wreath on a tray makes it easier to move about.

    The Advent wreath is a Christian symbol reminding us that Jesus is the light of the world who dispels darkness from our lives. When you gather to light the candle(s), darken the room if possible. Share your hopes for the festive season and pray together. Have a child do the lighting. This is an opportunity for youngsters to handle matches and fire under supervision.

    > First Sunday in Advent: Light one purple candle.
    > Second Sunday in Advent: Light two purple candles.
    > Third Sunday in Advent: Light two purple candles and the pink one.
    > Fourth Sunday in Advent: Light all four candles.
    > If you have a fifth candle (white) in the center of the wreath, light it on Christmas Eve.

- Create your own Christmas cards. No extraordinary artistic ability is needed to do this. Children's drawings have

great charm, and they will guarantee that your family's cards are originals. If you send a lot of cards, you'll probably want to choose one design and have it reproduced. This can be done inexpensively at a fast-print shop.
- Give a gift of yourself. Draw names in your family, but instead of buying gifts, give certificates stating some help you will give or some kindness you will do. For example: preparing a meal, doing a brother's or sister's household chores for a day, babysitting for a specified number of hours, loaning a favorite record or tape.
- For any difficult-to-buy-for person, consider donating money to a charity in that person's name. Choose charities that have significance to the one you are gifting. One man wrote to his father at Christmas and thanked him for helping with his education. He told his father he was giving a gift in his honor to help educate others. Then he made a donation to Operation Boot Strap, an organization that supplies materials to build schools in Africa. There are many charities from which to choose—some well-known and some little-known. Often one can be found right in your own community. To name just a few: a home for abused women and children, emergency food shelves, a historical restoration, a church building fund.
- Share your joy. Invite someone who would otherwise be alone for the holidays to take part in your Christmas celebrations.
- Have a nativity scene as a prominent part of your Christmas decorations. If you have a young child, set up a stable early in Advent and add the animals one by one. During the final week of Advent, the figures of Mary and Joseph approach the stable. Move them closer each day until, on Christmas Eve, they are part of the Nativity scene. On Christmas morning, place Jesus in the manger. Then come the shepherds who'd been told: "For to you is born this day in the city of David a Savior, who is Christ the Lord" (Luke 2:11, RSV).

10

Giving Lent a Chance

Easter Is Coming

In my growing-up years, the season of Lent meant having fish twice a week and praying the rosary every night. Also we went to the Stations of the Cross on Friday, and (as if these weren't observances enough!) we were expected to "give up" something. Invariably I decided to forgo candy and stuck each piece that came my way into a bag kept in my bottom dresser drawer. Back then, Lent officially ended on Holy Saturday noon. I remember sitting in the kitchen waiting out the minutes and finally the seconds until the hands on the electric wall clock touched 12:00. At that instant, I took my first exquisitely delicious bite from a piece of candy carefully selected from my six-week hoard. Lent was over. Alleluia! Alleluia!

Since then, Lenten practices and attitudes have changed. Now the emphasis is less on giving up and more on *giving of ourselves*. It's less on having rules imposed on us and more on *making personal decisions as to what will be spiritually enriching* for self and family. Although I don't champion the old style, there were some benefits to it. The rigors of Lent never failed to bring me to Easter with a sense that I had done something to prepare for the resurrection. I'd prayed and denied myself, and I was ready. With today's more relaxed attitude toward Lent, the question for us individually and as families is: How do we make Lent meaningful? What can we do to feel we are spiritually prepared for Easter and ready to celebrate it?

We can do a number of things, but as one mother with several years of parenting experience cautioned, "When you're introducing something to the family, don't try to do too much all at once. Start a tradition slowly, and add to it a little at a time." That's how it was with her family and the Easter tree.

The tree consists of three small tree branches stuck in a plaster-of-paris base. The first year, the mother and her two daughters decorated the tree with flowers they had made from paper and fabric. Over the years, they have made or collected other things that symbolize new life. These get hung on the tree each year in the same way that their Christmas ornaments get saved and reused. As the children grew older, they decorated Ukrainian eggs with symbols of Easter: crosses, a ladder for prayer, a rake for planting and harvesting.

Each year the family's Easter tree goes up on Ash Wednesday. It is a sign for them that Lent has arrived and they must decide what to do to prepare themselves for Easter.

Why Lent at All?

Lent originated as a period of final preparation for adults who wanted to be received into the Church. Those who made it were baptized during the Easter Vigil celebration. When adult conversion was no longer the norm, Lent remained as a time of renewal and repentance for the entire Church. The length of time for observing Lent has varied. For many years, it was a thirty-six-day period of fasting. About 800 A.D., four days were added, possibly as a reminder of the forty days Jesus fasted in the wilderness.

The word *Lent* comes from the Old English word *lencten*, which meant springtime. In the spring, nature comes to new life. In the resurrection, Jesus passed through death to life, revealing God's promise that at the end of life we too will have a new beginning, a time to look within and see what stands in the way of our being more caring people, more loving families. What holds us back? Jealousy? Anger? Self-pity? Whatever it is, we can work at changing during the forty days of Lent. As we die to our faults, we rise to what we can become as individuals and as a family.

Rich in Tradition

A look at customs from the past can generate ideas for observing Lent today. Although Lent begins on Ash Wednesday, Shrove Tuesday is sometimes celebrated. Its name comes from the old custom of confessing, or being *shriven*, on that day. In many countries and communities, Shrove Tuesday is a time of rejoicing. In southern Europe, it's the last day of the carnival season and corresponds to the Mardi Gras of the French and the Pancake Tuesday of the English. Why Pancake Tuesday? The custom of serving pancakes on Shrove Tuesday is believed to go back to the Christians who lived in the Roman Empire. During the entire season of Lent they ate no cheese, milk, cream, butter, eggs, or meat. The night before Ash Wednesday was the last chance to use up these foods, most of which were the ingredients for pancakes. If you serve pancakes on Shrove Tuesday, and the family asks "Why pancakes?" it's a springboard for talking about the meaning of Lent and what your family can do to make the season meaningful.

In our family, we find that attending Ash Wednesday church services is a good way to begin the Lenten journey. On the other hand, we have friends who commemorate the day by conducting their own services. Palms saved from the previous Palm Sunday are burned to make ashes. Family members use them to mark the sign of the cross on one another's forehead as a reminder to leave the past in ashes and come back to the Lord. A parent then reads the Scripture that cautions against making a public display of fasting and almsgiving, behavior that is unnecessary because "your Father who sees in secret will reward you" (Matthew 6:1-6, RSV). Afterward the family discusses what they are going to do to observe Lent.

A Time to Pray

Scripture readings at the beginning of Lent tell us Jesus turned from his everyday life and entered the desert, where he prayed and fasted. During the Lenten season, special emphasis is placed on prayer. Some families set aside time each day, or have a once-a-week "family time" during which they pray and take turns reading Scripture. The readings might take the place of grace at the evening meal. Remember that hunger makes both adults and children impatient and inattentive. With that in mind, keep the readings brief, or have them after you've eaten—possibly between the main course and dessert (if you have dessert in Lent).

Some churches publish suggested daily Scripture readings in their bulletins. If you don't have a guide, Jeremiah makes good reading in the early weeks of Lent. As Holy Week approaches, switch to the Gospel of John. Read without rushing, using a translation you feel is best for your family.

Although praying as a family is a bonding force, we also need to pray alone. Scripture tells us, "Go into your room and shut the door and pray to your Father" (Matthew 6:6, RSV). If you've been thinking of intensifying your prayer life and just haven't gotten to it, there is no better time than Lent. The six weeks of the season provide a time frame within which to make a plan. Maybe you'll want to try something innovative like keeping a journal or making a "Days of Lent Prayer Book"—a book with just forty pages on which you write, draw, or copy something that has spiritual meaning for you. The Lenten prayerbook is a project for children as well as adults. By occasionally looking back at where we've been, we get a better sense of our spiritual direction.

A Time to Fast

Self-denial is not much in favor in our culture, yet it's very much in keeping with the penitential character of Lent. The roots of fasting run deep in our Christian heritage. In the Old Testament, annual fasts mark disasters in Jewish history. Generally the fasts of our scriptural ancestors were strenuous, requiring abstinence from all food and drink. In the Hebrew Scriptures, there are also accounts of occasional fasts by individuals and groups. Such fasting gave expression to grief or penitence or was thought to be useful in securing God's help. The New Testament tells us that Jesus fasted, and we know that fasting was practiced in the early Church.

What is the value of fasting in contemporary life? Does denying ourselves food or drink serve any worthwhile purpose? It does if we see it as a way to strengthen our will, if we look at it as a means of simplifying our lives and eliminating the excesses. When we eat less, we realize that we normally consume more than we need for health and well-being. This may lead us to consider simplifying our lives in other ways as well.

Even though parents and children may fast on their own, it's especially rewarding to do it as a family. It gives a team spirit to the effort, and there's built-in support when the initial enthusiasm wanes, as it's sure to do. Everyone in the family should be involved in planning what to abstain from, and when and how the fasting is to be carried out. Children in preschool and the early grades need special consideration and support in following fasting guidelines. It's important that they be praised when they're successful, and not made to feel guilty when they have lapses. Following are some ways the family might decide to fast:

- Cut out between-meal snacks.
- Eliminate foods such as potato chips, pop, and sugary treats.
- Stop serving desserts.
- Once or twice a week, serve a simple meal that consists of soup or salad, bread, and a beverage. Donate the money saved to the needy.
- Serve meat half as often as usual.
- Follow the fasting regulations of your church.

When we think of "giving up" something for Lent, food necessarily comes to mind. But there are other ways of practicing self-denial that may be equally meaningful. We could give up some TV viewing time and spend it on a family activity or visiting someone who is lonely and alone; give up smoking and donate the money saved to a favorite charity; give up gossiping or being critical and see the rewards we reap. If we take such actions and discuss them with our children, they are encouraged to look at their own lives and do something that will make Lent meaningful for them.

A Time to Be Charitable

During Lent we're called to do works of charity. What we do will depend upon age, situation, and a host of other factors. But whoever we are and whatever our circumstance, we can find ways to reach out to others. Is there someone close to you who is troubled? Could you listen more attentively? Be more affectionate? Pray for that person's well-being? Seek outside guidance?

What could you do as a family to be more present to each other? More helpful? More loving?

Is there someone in your neighborhood who needs a ride to the store, a friendly visit, or an invitation to share a meal and spend some time with you and your family?

Could you join a worthy cause and commit yourself to giving time throughout the year?

Would it be possible to tithe during the six weeks of Lent and give the money to charity? Could you make a contribution in money or food to a needy family?

Lent is a time to give of our goods and of ourselves. Either way we are reaching out in charity. It is what Jesus did, and as Christ-followers we are called to do likewise.

The Week Called Holy

The final week of Lent is the only time of the year that's called Holy. Although churches hold special services that help us observe the events leading up to the resurrection, some families conduct their own observances. The highlight of the week for one family occurs on Holy Thursday when they have a Seder meal that incorporates the traditions of the Jewish Passover and the Last Supper. It's a meal to which they invite guests and have ritualistic prayers before serving radishes—which are their bitter herbs—dipped in salt water that symbolizes tears. Historically the Passover meal was festive, and this family tries to keep it that way. They may have lamb or chicken stuffed with matzos. Only unleavened bread is served, and there is always fresh fruit along with wine for the adults and grape juice for the children. When the meal is over, they say more prayers and end the evening with singing.

After the warmth and sharing of Holy Thursday comes the bleakness of the crucifixion on Good Friday. Often it's a day that children have off from school. When ours were young, we set aside an hour in the afternoon to commemorate the day and make it sacred in our own fashion. It was a quiet time in which to pray together and then to draw or paint or listen to music that inspired reflection. Such activities seemed to hold more meaning for the children than going to a church service that often lasted longer than they could sit still.

And Then Comes Easter

When children are young, they cannot be expected to understand the resurrection, and certainly not its implications. Even for adults, it remains the central mystery of our faith. But from the time our children were able to toddle about, they associated Easter with happiness because that was the day the Easter bunny came. Their gleeful smiles and shouts of delight at discovering their hidden baskets expressed the joy that Easter is all about. As the children got older and we observed Lent in various ways, they grew in understanding of the resurrection, but traditions die hard. Although now in their late teens and early twenties, they still search the house for goody-filled baskets on Easter morning. And they find them! Even new shoes and clothes have a certain relevance to Easter in that they too are signs of change. And in a sense, new beginnings.

When we truly understand Easter, we know that the resurrection is more than a single event that happened some 2,000 years ago. There are resurrections occurring all around us—in winter turning to spring, in the paralyzed teen finding life worth living, in the recovered mental patient coping with the world again, in the alcoholic overcoming dependency. Resurrection occurs anytime despair turns to hope and hate turns to love.

If we've spent the days of Lent fasting, praying, and making a greater-than-usual effort to show concern for one another, we come to Easter with a special sense of joy. But to know that joy, we have to give Lent a chance.

Some Things to Try

- Plant an amaryllis bulb on Ash Wednesday. The bulb will take five or six weeks to flower. If all goes well, it should have large, fragrant blossoms by Easter. Put the bulb in an attractive pot with plenty of soil, place it near a window, and water it regularly. Letting children help plant the bulb and tend it as it grows helps them experience Lent as a time of waiting and preparing. After the bulb has flowered, it can be wrapped in newspaper and kept in a cool, dark place until the following year. It then resumes its symbolism of death and resurrection.
- Dye Easter eggs. In ancient times, eggs were a symbol of spring and fertility. This was because an egg appears dead even while it contains life. During medieval times, the Easter egg became a symbol of the tomb out of which Jesus rose to new life.
- Join in Operation Rice Bowl. This program is designed to help feed the hungry in this country and around the world. Those who participate are asked to eat a simple meal of soup or salad one day a week during Lent and to

put the money that is saved into a cardboard rice bowl provided by the program. Children may even dip into their pockets and piggy banks to make contributions on their own. Usually entire parishes sign up to take part. If your parish is not already participating, more information may be obtained by writing to:

    Operation Rice Bowl
    Catholic Relief Services
    1011 First Avenue
    New York, NY 10020

- Begin some Lenten practices that will become traditions in your family. Remember that you can start small and each year add to what you do. If having an entire Seder meal on Holy Thursday seems like too much, serve a Passover Salad with your dinner. It's simple enough that children can help with it, or make it themselves.

PASSOVER SALAD

6 medium apples, grated or chopped fine
½ cup raisins
½ cup chopped nuts
1 tsp. cinnamon
¼ cup wine

    Mix and serve. The sweet taste is a reminder of the slavery that is now ended.

- Share Easter breads. Invite friends over, and ask them each to bring a special bread to share. Have wine or juice to go with the bread. The sharing of bread and wine is a means of carrying the symbol of the Eucharist into the home.
- Have a family reconciliation service at home. Pattern it after the service in Chapter 8 ("Forgiving and Forgetting") under *Some Things to Try*.

11

Doing Something About Hunger

Face-to-face with the Problem

Like everyone else who watches the evening news on television or reads the daily paper, I knew about hunger in our country. But for me, the problem lacked reality until I became involved with Loaves and Fishes, an interdenominational effort to feed the hungry.

The first time I went to the aging parochial school where the meals were served, I came face-to-face with people who did not take food for granted. There were oldsters who saved part of their meal, tucking a slice of bread or a cookie in a pocket or purse as insurance against tomorrow's hunger. While waiting in line, young adults angrily complained about not being able to find work. Stubble-faced drifters and bag ladies were part of the crowd. So, too, were families. Weary parents with defeat in their eyes looked as if they'd given up hope that life would ever be better for them or for their children. Whatever the circumstances that brought people to Loaves and Fishes, all were hungry. Many came early, even in the winter, and waited in line an hour or more.

Each time I volunteered, I wondered what it would be like if our roles were reversed. What if I were waiting instead of serving? What if I were never sure where my next meal was coming from and had to watch my children go to bed hungry?

The Extent of the Problem

No one knows precisely how many people suffer from hunger in this country. Government task forces come up with much lower figures than do citizen groups. One way to judge the extent of the problem is to look at the figures on poverty, because hunger is poverty's companion. The figure set as a poverty level income changes from year to year. In 1983 it was $12,000 for a family of four.[1] The last census classified 31.8 million Americans as impoverished. That's a whopping 14 percent of the population![2]

In every family's budget there are fixed outlays for items such as housing and utilities. One variable in the budget is food. Poor people save money by eating starchy, "filling" foods that are relatively inexpensive, or by eating less, or by not eating at all. A Gallup poll taken in 1984 indicated that 20 percent of Americans at times do not have enough money for food—up from 14 percent ten years earlier.[3]

Although the figures on hunger in this country are unsettling, globally they are staggering. Out of a world population of 4.5 billion, some 700 million are seriously and chronically malnourished. Of these, half are children. This year alone, roughly 10 million people will die, and malnutrition will be a major contributing factor.[4]

Sometimes the hungry in our midst go unnoticed because they don't fit the stereotype of the needy. They may have a house to live in. Perhaps they are adequately clothed and own a car. Although by appearances they are comfortably well off, they can be in such bad financial shape that the result is hunger, or at best an inadequate diet. Such is frequently the case of women who are left to raise a family alone. When marriages end, women stand a fifty-fifty chance of living in poverty.[5]

One such case is Susan, the divorced mother of five. When her husband remarried and left the state, months passed without a support check from him. Although Susan went to work immediately, the only job she was able to find paid just under $750 a month. The single supplement to her income was about $50 a month in food stamps. After paying the mortgage and utilities, she had $300 left to cover medical bills, insurance, transportation, clothing, and food for six people. When she signed her children up for free lunch programs at school, the principal thought she was joking. Susan says, "Three years ago I helped raise money for our church food bank. Now I'm in the line."[6]

Social Programs to the Rescue

One of the things that has helped sustain those living at or near poverty is the food stamp program. In the late 1960s, a physicians' report touched off an outcry about hunger in this country. The result was legislation for improved food assistance—in particular the food stamp and the child nutrition programs that supplemented the diets of some 20 million Americans. Although the number of people at or below the poverty line fell only slightly, the incidence and severity of hunger dropped sharply. But profound cuts were later made in social welfare benefits. By the summer of 1981, $1.7 billion had been lopped off the food stamp program; this took 480,000 families off food stamps and reduced benefits for an additional 270,000 others. Along with the budget cuts in social welfare came an unprecedented increase in peacetime defense spending: $1.5 *trillion* over five years.[7] Of every federal dollar spent, 41 cents goes for national defense, whereas only 22 cents goes for social programs.[8]

Is there a connection between defense spending and hunger? Dwight Eisenhower, former general and president, stated, "Every gun that is made, every warship launched, every rocket fired signifies in the final sense, a theft from those who hunger and are not fed."[9]

Of course there are bound to be abuses in any kind of large-scale, government-funded spending. The food stamp program is no exception insofar as greed, not need, motivates some people to take advantage of the system. But the good that various food assistance programs have done for the hungry outweighs the costs. People who have proper nutrition are brighter, healthier, and more productive. Although some undeserving people get food stamps, many of those who are eligible don't even take part in the program. Only about 60 percent of the people entitled to food stamps actually receive them. The other 40 percent aren't aware that they qualify, feel embarrassed to use food stamps, or are discouraged by the long forms and red tape required to get them.[10]

The Power of the Pen

We've been told to write to our government representatives so often on so many different issues that the advice seems trite. Yet it's within the power of anyone capable of writing a letter to do something about hunger. Letters that effectively communicate our concerns become weapons in the fight against hunger. "Someone who sits down and writes a letter about hunger . . . almost literally has to be saving a life," states Paul Simon, a U.S. Representative from Illinois.[11]

James Wright, a Representative from Texas, bolsters this position by stating:

> If you are wondering whether it is really worthwhile to communicate your views to your senators or representatives in Congress, consider this fact: others who disagree with you are doing so constantly. Lobbyists and well-paid public relations people attempt daily to persuade members of Congress that not only votes but public opinion lies on their side.[12]

If we are to truly attend to the needs of the disadvantaged, we are obliged to work at changing the social conditions that cause them. For far too long, there has been a gap between the way concerned citizens feel about the impoverished and the position our government representatives take. Our task is to prod them toward more permanent and more dignified solutions to poverty than

handouts. When writing to a representative the following guidelines help express ideas and concerns effectively:
- Be brief. An effective letter can be as short as two or three well-thought-out sentences. Rarely should it exceed one full page.
- Concentrate on one issue per letter. Ask for specific action.
- Express your own views in your own words. The more individual the letter, the more attention it will receive.
- Be considerate. Don't threaten or make demands. *Request* your representative's consideration of your views.
- Don't hesitate to write. It's the job of those elected to public office to listen to the views of their constituents.

We Can and Must

The problem of hunger is so large and complex that any attempt on our part to alleviate it may seem futile. But in this, as in many other situations, it's still better to light one little candle than to curse the darkness.

Some 200 Lutheran young people found that they could better serve the needs of the hungry collectively than would have been possible individually. On two and a half acres of land donated by farmers in southwestern Wisconsin, they raised seven tons of vegetables that were distributed to the hungry in Milwaukee's inner city. The project was dubbed "Joseph's Granary" in reference to the Old Testament figure who ministered to the hunger of God's chosen people.

In order to sensitize themselves to the needs of the poor, some individuals and entire families fast. Fasting takes different forms. Some people give up a meal a week or consume only liquids one day a month. Others make fasting a way of life by always eating small helpings and forgoing seconds. A young woman who took part in a thirty-hour fast said, "I learned a lot about how it feels to be hungry. How can you work, learn, or love when your only concern is with filling your stomach?" Although her experience gave her a valuable insight, fasting with consistency and perseverance is a better way to identify with the chronically hungry than a once-in-a-lifetime marathon fast.

Whether it be personally relieving someone's hunger or assailing the forces that create the situations in which it can exist, our faith obliges us to act. As John F. Kennedy said in his inaugural address, "If a free society cannot help the many who are poor, it cannot save the few who are rich." Individually and collectively we can do something about hunger. And indeed we must.

Some Things to Try

- Join Bread for the World, a Christian citizens' movement against hunger. Begun in 1974, the organization prods members of Congress to adopt policies favorable to feeding the hungry at home and overseas. For membership information write to:
    Bread for the World
    6411 Chillum Place, N.W.
    Washington, DC 20012
- Contribute to, or start, a food collection drive in your church. Canned and boxed goods can be left in collection baskets at the door or—as is done in some churches—brought to the altar.
- Plant a garden and share the produce. So much the better if you have a plot of land, but it's not altogether necessary. It's possible to have a garden with no more than a sunny balcony, a windowsill, or a back step. This limited gardening is done in containers—plastic tubs, pails, cans; even baskets and boxes lined with plastic trash bags will do.
- Volunteer at the local food stamp advocacy program in your community. If there is none, work with others toward establishing one.
- Feed the birds. It is something children can do, and it teaches them to be concerned about all living creatures.

- Pray daily for the blessing of food. Mealtime is the ideal opportunity to turn to God as a family and give thanks for the food that nourishes our bodies. It's also a time to pray for guidance in trying to meet the needs of the hungry.

12

Touching with Love

I Think She Likes Me

When our daughter Ann was in the fifth grade, she had a teacher I'll call Miss Allen. Exaggerated stories of Miss Allen's tyranny became legendary, and new students entered her class with foreboding. Gradually, however, their fear turned to respect. Miss Allen expected a lot out of her students—more than many thought they had to give—and she got it. Receiving an *A* from her was a source of immense pride and satisfaction.

Ann's diligence in Miss Allen's class was rewarded with good marks. And as fall turned to winter, it became obvious that she felt something more than respect for the exacting Miss Allen. She had, in fact, grown quite fond of her. I didn't realize just how much she wanted that fondness returned until one day she came home from school and, with a happy sigh, confided, "At last I think Miss Allen likes me."

"Why do you say that?" I asked.

"Because," Ann replied, "when she walked past my desk today, she touched my head."

A Necessity for Survival

Touch communicates as surely as words, and sometimes more effectively. A kindly hand placed on the head, a pat on the back, a gentle squeeze of the hand—each conveys a message of caring and warmth that we may be unwilling, or unable, to express in words. Often in a grief situation a warm embrace is more supportive and nurturing than the most earnest murmurings of sympathy. Likewise, in a joyous situation, an exuberant hug expresses our shared delight better than anything we might say. Touch is more than just an "extra" way to communicate. It is basic to our relating to one another—so basic, in fact, that infants must be lovingly touched if they are to survive.

"Being touched and caressed, being massaged, is food for the infant. Food as necessary as minerals, vitamins, and protein," writes gynecologist and obstetrician Frederick Leboyer. "Deprived of this food, the name of which is love, babies would rather die. And they often do."[1]

During the 1800s, more than half the infants died during their first year from a disease called *marasmus*, a Greek word meaning "wasting away." As late as the 1920s, the death rate in the U.S. from this disorder was nearly 100 percent for babies under a year old who lived in orphanages. Those statistics began to change when an American doctor brought the idea of tender, loving care back with him from Germany. At a children's clinic in Dusseldorf, the doctor noticed a fat, grandmotherly woman walking around with a particularly scrawny baby on her hip. Inquiring about the woman, the doctor was told, "Oh, that is Old Anna. When we have done everything we can medically for a baby, and it is still not doing well, we turn it over to her, and she is always successful."[2] The lifesaving treatment Anna gave did not require a medical degree. She simply caressed, rocked, and stroked the babies. She gave them the tenderness they needed in order to survive.

A baby's need for such care seems obvious to us today, but as late as the mid-1930s the dogmatic teachings of Emmett Holt, Sr.—the leading child expert of his day—were steadfastly in place. He believed in abolishing the cradle and feeding by the clock. He did not believe in picking a baby up when it cried or in handling it too much, fearing the result would be a spoiled child. According to Professor Holt's philosophy, the concept of tender, loving care was unscientific. But a study undertaken to discover the cause of marasmus revealed that infants were dying from the "scientific" methods advocated by the professor. Marasmus, it was found, frequently occurred in the "best" home and institutions. Although the environments were comfortable and sterile, the babies were dying from want of being picked up, carried around, and nurtured by a loving touch. When "mothering" was introduced to Bellevue Hospital in New York, mortality rates for infants under one year fell from about 35 percent to less than 10 percent.[3]

Babies have an endearingly soft and cuddly appeal. For a great many of us, it's difficult to keep from touching them, at least by the time they're big enough that we aren't afraid they'll break. But as infants grow into toddlers, they no longer need, or want, to be handled as much. By the time they become teenagers, we might give up hugging them altogether and find few other ways to express our love through touch. Could this lack of loving touch be a factor in the disintegration of the family? Family counselor Helen Colton believes it is. She says, "My years of counseling and teaching families have taught me that it is unlikely that a child or spouse living in a tactile, loving environment would feel any need to take off through running away, using drugs or divorcing."[4] Therapist Arthur Janov adds to her observation when he writes, "Cults and related movements offer a new family. They provide the follower with new people to worry about him, to offer him advice, to cry with him and, importantly, *to hold and touch him*. Those are unbeatable attractions."[5]

Old Patterns Can Be Broken

If touch is so important in families, why don't we do more of it? Like so much of our behavior, we learned it in childhood. "People who were not touched as children often have trouble touching their own children," writes psychologist Jules Older.[6] Such people will be prone to offer a cookie or cracker to a child who is hurt or lonely when what the child really wants is the warmth of touch, the communication of love that comes from being rocked or held close. Although home is the place where behavior patterns are formed, it is also the place where old patterns can be broken and replaced by new ones.

The younger the child, the easier it is to adopt a new way of relating. With teenagers, it becomes more difficult, but it's not impossible. If we suddenly smother them with hugs or bombard them with affectionate pats, we'll probably get an irritated "What's with you?" But as we send them off to school in the morning, we can pat a shoulder or give a squeeze around the waist. Even the most ardent hands-off family member probably won't be able to resist a good back rub. Whatever touching we do needs to fit our own personal style and be something we're comfortable with. "We need not be afraid to touch, to feel, to show emotion," states the exuberant writer and speaker Leo Buscaglia, whose audiences line up to be hugged. "The easiest thing in the world to be is what you are, what you feel."[7]

Touch Gone Wrong

Touch in families can go wrong. Terribly wrong. Some parents cite "spare the rod and spoil the child" (based on Proverbs 13:24) to justify severely beating their children. Others turn the gift of touch into the perversion of sexual abuse. Incest, the darkest of all family secrets, has been brought out of the closet. No one really knows the extent of the problem, except that it is enormous and likely to be more shocking as new statistics are revealed.

It was once widely held that the greatest sexual abusers of children were strangers who lured them with candy and other rewards. It is now known that 80 percent of the sexual assaults on children are done by someone they know and trust, usually a family member.[8] Because children have unrestrained love and unquestioning trust, this is the ultimate betrayal. One study estimates that nationally at least 45,000 children are sexually abused each year in incidents ranging from fondling to various forms of intercourse. For every case that's reported, it's believed there are 2 to 25 that go unreported.[9]

Often child molesters tell the child that what they are doing together is their "secret." As such, it is not to be shared with anyone, not even parents. Perhaps one of the best ways to protect our children from sexual abuse is to tell them at a very early age that there should be no secrets they can't tell us—even if someone warns that something bad will happen if they do. Then if a child does reveal a secret that we may not want to hear, we must listen—and listen well—because young children rarely make up stories about being sexually molested.

Another way to protect children from potential molestation is to talk about what is good touching and what is not. Without being alarmists, we can tell children that if anyone touches them in a way that frightens, hurts, or confuses them, we want to be told—even if the touching is done by someone the child knows and loves. But often because of shame or confusion or guilt, children refuse to talk about the violation of their bodies. When the words go unspoken, behavior can sometimes provide the clues. A specialist in treating child abuse cases suggests that in children under eight, there might be regressive behavior such as bedwetting, clinging, whining, and baby talk. There might also be constant physical complaints (a veiled way of drawing attention to the problem) and explicit sexual talk or unusually precocious sexual play. Older children might become withdrawn, depressed, or show self-destructive tendencies.[10] Such behavior is not in itself a sign of sexual abuse, but may be a warning that something is seriously amiss in the child's life. The cause, not the symptoms, needs to be dealt with.

With the increased attention being given to child abuse, the numbers of agencies offering help are increasing as well. In communities both large and small, the first call for help can be to the police. Referrals are then made to other helping agencies and organizations.

The Gift of Touch

Good touching is a gift—a gift we can give to one another. Touching is a means of expressing empathy and comfort. If you've ever visited a nursing home with a young child in tow, you may have had residents reaching out to touch the child on the head or clasp a hand. That used to happen to us on our visits to "Great Grandma," and I was moved at how the elderly in the nursing home where she lived hungered for the touch of another human. That same hunger is by no means confined to the walls of nursing homes.

Everywhere there are people yearning for a touch that tells them they are valued. A psychologist wrote about Sally, a battering mother who went into a treatment program and developed a trusting relationship with her social worker. During one of their interviews, Sally broke into tears, and the worker put a sympathetic hand on her shoulder. Later Sally was to say, "When Mrs. D. put her hand on my shoulder, I felt a sense of hope for the first time in my life. . . ."[11]

Our touch may never have such a profound effect on anyone, but there are people in our lives who will be nurtured by our reaching out to them. One man told of abruptly losing a job he'd held for fifteen years. The loss filled him with such a sense of failure that he felt unworthy even to be touched. Some months later, the man got another job and regained his self-esteem. In talking about the experience, he credited his wife and children with getting him through that tough time by not withholding their hugs and other signs of affection when he himself had none to give.

We can find many opportunities in our daily lives to turn the gift of touch into the gift of love. And when we do, we will be enriched as surely as those to whom we have reached out.

Some Things to Try

- Hold hands around the table while saying grace. It adds a new dimension to praying together as a family.

- Give one another gentle back rubs. When one of our sons was in the upper elementary grades, he used to have difficulty falling asleep, especially after playing in competitive sports. A back rub at bedtime proved to be a cure for his insomnia.
- Go one step further and give massages. An excellent book with easy-to-follow directions is Armand Maanum's *The Complete Book of Swedish Massage* (Winston Press).
- Have a rocking chair in the house. Rocking is a wonderful way to soothe an infant, and it's also relaxing for the one doing the rocking. Rocking need not stop with infancy. We found that, until the children grew too big to fit in our laps, rocking comforted a tired, frustrated child and helped take the sting out of hurt feelings and disappointments.
- Give young children lots of opportunities for touching. That is one of the principal ways they learn about their environment. Children like and need the experience of playing with water, sand, dirt. It's the way they make discoveries about the properties of various elements of nature. Given a small amount of guidance, children can handle rather delicate objects with care. When our children were about three, we began letting them drink from the good stem goblets at holiday dinners and on other special occasions. This was a special treat, and not one of them ever broke a goblet. Of course, if something is so valuable it would be catastrophic if it were broken, children should not be allowed to touch it.
- Do you spank to discipline? If you do, consider whether there might be a more positive way to get your child to behave. Spanking sends the message that when you're angry it's okay to physically strike out at someone. Helping children feel good about themselves and giving them positive strokes when they do something praiseworthy helps eliminate the need for discipline as forceful as spanking.
- If you have evidence that someone is physically or sexually abusing a child, report it to the police, school, or a social service agency. Children have a right to be safe, and

we who are brothers and sisters in Christ have an obligation to help guarantee it.

13

Accepting Death as a Part of Life

Mud on His Face

When one of our sons was five, he said that when he died and "got buried," he hoped it wasn't raining. I asked why, and he answered, "Because when I come back to life, I don't want to be walking around with mud on my face." After I told him that he could always wash the mud off, he went happily on his way.

This exchange happened in the Easter season, and apparently he made a connection between his death and what he'd heard about the resurrection. Even so, his remark took me by surprise. Children's comments about death have a way of doing that. We think it's a subject that's beyond them, that death is something they don't think about yet. But how could they not?

Children see death on TV and hear about it in church; they read about it in fairy tales and listen in when adults are talking about it. Their first experience of actually seeing something dead will probably involve a dead animal or bird. Curiosity leads them to examine the remains and ask questions. Although their interest may be distasteful to us, we should not be surprised by it. Young children wonder about all of life—and death is a part of life. We can let their interest be a reminder that it's as natural to die as it is to be born and that we cannot have one experience without the other.

If we want to deal effectively with our children's curiosity about death, there is one prerequisite: We must have examined our own beliefs and fears about it. Are we afraid of dying? Do we believe in an afterlife? If we were told we had only a short time to live, would it change the way we are living? When we've accepted our own mortality and its implications for living, we've laid the groundwork for discussing death with our children.

How Children View Death

The way children view death changes as they mature. The following guidelines are helpful in understanding their reactions at various ages, but it's important to remember that children mature at individual rates. As in all developmental guidelines, these ages should be regarded as approximate.

Up to age three, children tend to see death as a temporary separation. If Daddy dies, he has only gone away for a while and will return. When the deceased doesn't come back—whether it is a parent or a beloved pet—the child feels abandoned and unloved.

Between ages three and five, death is seen as temporary and reversible. In their play, children "die" and promptly pop back to life. Watching TV cartoon characters get flattened by a steamroller or blown apart and miraculously become whole again tends to reinforce the notion that death is a temporary condition.

After age six, children sense death's permanence. Although they may realize that all living things die, they still do not see death as personal. It's mostly something that happens to animals and old people. At about age eight, many children have an intense interest in what happens after death. Because so much about death remains a mystery, there are times when we will have to respond, "I don't know." Rather than disappointing the child, our honest, nondefensive admission is apt to make us all the more credible.

By age nine or ten, children comprehend that death is irreversible and that they, too, will die one day. Some begin to develop philosophical views about life and death. As youngsters move into the teen years, they often become intrigued with seeking the meaning of life. Some teens disguise their fear of death by taking unnecessary chances with their lives. They might drive recklessly or attempt daring physical feats. Confirming their control over mortality is a way of overcoming their fears.

Strangers to Death

Although children are exposed to a great deal of death on television (approximately 10,000 killings from birth to age 21),[1] they will have little personal experience with it. It's entirely possible for children today to reach adulthood without ever having anyone close to them die. This is a situation quite different from what it was at the turn of the century. Back then, children under the age of 15 accounted for over 50 percent of all deaths. There's hardly a child who would not have experienced the death of at least one friend, cousin, brother, or sister. Today only 5 percent of the population dies between birth and age 15. Those 65 or over account for 67 percent of all deaths.

The Death of a Pet

The one experience of loss that many children share, and over which they grieve, is the death of a cherished pet. When a cat or dog dies, it's tempting to try to console the child by offering to get another one. But psychologist Haim Ginott cautions against quickly replacing what the child has lost. If this is done, he says a child " . . . may conclude that the loss of loved ones is of no great importance; that love may easily be transferred and loyalty easily shifted. A child should not be deprived of his right to grieve and to mourn . . . . The child's humanity is deepened, and his character ennobled, when he can lament the end of life and love."[2]

Many children are helped to deal with a pet's death and their own sadness if they take part in the animal's burial. When one of our son's pet gerbils died, he took it upon himself to put the gerbil in a box and bury it under one of the pines in the backyard. Some children find it therapeutic to make a marker and put it on the pet's grave. It's a way of helping them express the love they had for the pet, which in turn helps them work through their sadness.

A Death in the Family

Although the odds are against it, young children do sometimes experience a death in the family. In the shock and confusion that follow, it might seem like a good idea to send a child off to visit relatives or friends. But those who have expertise in working with the grieving say that, for the most part, children are better served by staying at home. Even very young children who do not understand the full implications of death are aware that something serious is going on. This is a time when they need familiar surroundings and close contact with family members. A lot of touching, holding, and hugging helps communicate to children that they will be cared for even though their lives are changing. The closeness of familiar and caring people lessens their fear of abandonment and other stresses they are likely to experience.

Grandma Is Not Sleeping

When talking to children about death, avoid euphemisms. Imagine yourself as a small child hearing someone say, "Grandma has gone to her eternal rest." Because children take things literally, you might well confuse death with sleep. The result of such confusion could be fear of going to bed or taking naps. Similarly, if a child hears that someone "went away" or "passed on," it suggests that death is not final and that the dead person will return. However unintentionally we lead children to such a belief, we are doing them a disservice. Although there may be something cold and terribly final about the words "dead" and "died," they are still the best ones to use when talking to children about death.

Should Children Attend Funerals?

There is a consensus among authorities that a child who can sit quietly in church, or attend other social functions with the family, should be invited—but never forced—to attend the funeral. Likewise, a child should be invited to view the body.

It's well to remember that young children have no innate fears concerning the dead. Their feelings are conditioned by the way people around them react. Children going to their first funeral should be prepared for what will occur during and after the services. They need to be aware that on such a sad occasion people express their sorrow in various ways and that some will be crying. Experiencing the mourning and the ritual of the funeral while surrounded by family and friends helps children accept the reality of death. Ideally, a child should have some part to play in the funeral. A four-year-old might, for example, help arrange flowers. An older child might pass out prayer cards or show mourners to their seats.

Working Through Grief

Grief is the cost of commitment, the price we pay for having loved. The grieving process is something everyone who has suffered the death of a loved one must go through if he or she is to pick up the pieces and go on living a full and normal life. By expressing our sorrow openly, we show children it is all right to cry and feel sad.

Children who show little immediate grief may lead us to think they are unaffected by the loss. Some mental health experts believe that children are not mature enough to work through a deeply felt loss until they are teenagers. Thus young children are apt to express their sadness on and off for a long time, and often at unexpected moments. Other family members might find it painful to have wounds reopened, but children need understanding and support to complete their grieving.

Dealing with anger and guilt is a large part of working through grief. These are feelings shared by adults and children. There may be anger at the dead person for causing so much sorrow, or anger at the doctors and nurses, or maybe even anger at ourselves for not being able to prevent the death. Although we may know intellectually that our feelings are irrational, our emotions take on a life of their own. Accepting that anger is a natural part of grief is a first step toward getting rid of it. Some grieving children express their anger in words or aggressive behavior, while others turn it inward and become withdrawn. If withdrawal leads to a prolonged depression, a child may require counseling.

The death of a loved one fills us adults with questions of "Why did I . . . ?" and "Why didn't I . . . ?" Children, too, must deal with guilt that can do serious emotional damage if it is not talked about. Roger was six when he walked into the room where his father had just had a fatal heart attack. Although his mother screamed for Roger to go to the neighbors for help, the boy couldn't move. Later, he told his older sister, "Daddy died because I couldn't do anything."[3]

Young children have difficulty understanding cause-and-effect relationships. They may think their angry thoughts caused the death, or that it was brought on by something they did or didn't do. One mother explained how her son thought the lemonade he made for his grandmother caused her heart attack. The boy spent many anguished months keeping his guilt and fear to himself. It wasn't until studying about poisons in a junior high science class that he learned the lemonade could not possibly have killed his grandmother. Only then did he tell his mother the secret he'd been carrying and how relieved he felt once he knew the truth.

When a death occurs in the family, children need to be given the facts simply and honestly. Questions should be encouraged so as to clear up mistaken notions. Accompanying explanations with a hug or some other affectionate gesture helps offset anxiety. Worries about abandonment are common. In the weeks and months following a death, children need many assurances that they are loved and will be cared for.

Being Prepared

One of the kindest and most forward-thinking things we can do for our families is to make out a will. Like many young parents, Herb and I thought there was plenty of time for such matters. We kept putting it off until one of our children asked, "What would happen to us kids if you and Dad both died?" That question prompted us to act.

The drafting of our will required only one visit to the lawyer's office. After the visit, we sat down with the children and told them the provisions we were considering if both of us were to die. They were sober faced as they agreed that the aunts and uncles we had in mind were good choices to care for them if it came to that. We also explained that there would be money for their care and college educations, which seemed to relieve them greatly. Finally, we told them that in the event of our deaths, we wanted to make donations of any usable organs. It made us feel good, we said, to know that our eyes might give someone the gift of sight or our heart extend another's life. When the final draft of the will arrived, we told each child where it could be found if it was needed.

Making a will is just one of the practical matters that families need to deal with. In writing about her experiences as a young widow, Lynn Caine makes a strong case for a Contingency Day—a day set aside once each year to review the financial state of the family. What would be the agenda for such a day? "They [the parents] could discuss steps to be taken if either husband or wife should die in the next twelve months. How much money the surviving spouse and children would have to live on. What changes in life-style

would be necessary. Such a discussion, in the natural context of family life, would minimize the later trauma of finding oneself a widow or widower."[4] Following are some steps to take to ease the burden that will fall on survivors:
- Write down what funeral arrangements you want. If you own a burial plot, note its location and attach the ownership documents to your arrangements. If you want to be cremated, specify what is to be done with the ashes.
- Attach your will to any insurance policies you own. Include the names and addresses of agents to be contacted.
- List bank accounts, and tell where bankbooks are kept.
- Prepare a list of any holdings of stocks, bonds, mutual funds, real estate, or other forms of property. Indicate where securities and deeds are, when you bought them, and what you paid. This will help in filing inheritance tax returns.
- Give details of any debts, such as your home mortgage or car.
- If you own a home, indicate when and where payments must be made on your homeowners' insurance policy and property taxes.

Taking care of such concerns is far from a morbid concentration on death. Rather, it is an expression of love and concern for family and friends. In facing the inevitability of our own deaths, we find the strength and courage to get on with making the most out of the time we have on this earth.

"It is the denial of death that is partially responsible for people living empty, purposeless lives; for when you live as if you'll live forever, it becomes too easy to postpone the things you know that you must do," writes Elisabeth Kübler-Ross, who is renowned for her research on death and dying. "You live your life in preparation for tomorrow or in remembrance of yesterday, and meanwhile, each today is lost. In contrast, when you fully understand that each day you awaken could be the last you have, you take the time *that day* to grow, to become more of who you really are, to reach out to other human beings."[5]

Some Things to Try

- Discuss death with children at times when there is no personal emotional involvement. If you live in a climate where there are marked seasonal changes, go for walks in the spring and the fall. Talk about death of plants and animals in nature. Television offers many opportunities to talk about death. If some well-known person dies and the event is covered in the news, you might talk about the causes of death and how people live on through their children, through contributions they may have made to society, and in the memories of those who knew them. Not the least, talk about death as a passage from life as we know it to a new life with God. Referring to that life, Scripture tells us: "God will wipe away every tear from their eyes, and death will be no more, neither shall there be mourning nor crying nor pain anymore" (Revelation 21:4, RSV).
- Face the inevitability of your own death and make decisions that will otherwise fall to others. If—in the event of terminal illness—you do not want to futilely have your death prolonged, a living will can be made. Such a will, along with additional information on the rights of the dying, can be obtained by writing to:
    Concern For Dying
    250 West 57th Street
    New York, NY 10019
- Acquaint yourself with the many good books available on the subject of death. For children, there are books of fiction for the preschool age through the teen years that deal realistically yet sensitively with the subject. For adults, there are a number of books that give an in-depth treatment of the emotional and practical aspects of death and the grieving process. Ask a librarian to direct you to those books best suited to your needs and to help children find books at their interest level. Herb and I created a giftbook to be given to anyone who is grieving. *Beyond Sorrow: Reflections on Death and Grief* is available from Winston Press.

- Be informed about donating organs. This option is unappealing to some, but those who see it as an opportunity to serve the needs of others after death should take steps to ensure that their wishes are honored. Many states now have donor forms on the back of drivers' licenses. There is also a Uniform Donor Card that is designed for the donor's wallet and in most states is a legal document. Copies of the Uniform Donor Card may be obtained without charge from
  Eye Bank Association of America
  3195 Maplewood Avenue
  Winston-Salem, NC 27103
 and from
  Living Bank
  Hermann Professional Building
  P.O. Box 6725
  Houston, TX 77005

14

Going Forth

A Mission to Fulfill

The Japanese social reformer Kagawa wrote:

> I read once
> In a book
> That a man
> Called Christ
> Went about
> Doing good
> It distresses me
> That I am
> So easily satisfied
> With just
> Going about.

Although we may nod appreciatively at the words that spin out an insight so smoothly, many of us get so caught up in the demands of parenting and earning a living that we balk at having to extend ourselves further. If the world needs changing, someone else will have to do it! Yet by the fact of our birth, we have already changed the world: We added one more human life to it. The question thus becomes, What changes will we continue to effect? Will we go about doing good, or will we simply go about?

According to the renowned psychiatrist Viktor Frankl, the primary motivation for all of us is finding a meaning in life. His dehumanizing experiences in a Nazi concentration camp crystallized his belief that "everyone has his own specific vocation or mission in life; we each must carry out a concrete assignment that demands fulfillment. Therein we cannot be replaced, nor can our life be repeated. Thus everyone's task is as unique as his specific opportunity to implement it."[1]

Others may do the same kind of work that we do, live on the same block, or even belong to the same family, but they don't think our thoughts or have our talents. They can't dream our dreams or live our lives. The task for each of us is to look at ourselves and ask, "What are *my* abilities? What are *my* interests? What can *I* do to follow the scriptural imperative to 'Use for the good of others the special gift [I have] received from God'?" (1 Peter 4:10, TEV).

The Most Terrible Want of All

Mother Teresa of Calcutta believes that whatever our gifts or talents, we all have a single mission. That mission is to love. In working with the poorest of the poor, she sees incredible poverty, yet to her there is a kind of suffering that's worse than being without material goods. That is the suffering that comes from being rejected, from not belonging anywhere. "Loneliness and the feeling of being unwanted is," she says, "the most terrible want of all."[2]

We don't have to go far to find people who would benefit from a friendly smile, an encouraging word, a helping hand. Perhaps we won't have to go beyond our own home. Surely we won't have to go farther than our neighborhood or workplace. Although most of us aren't going to have the opportunity to be a Good Samaritan like the one in the Bible, our compassion and understanding can be as helpful as binding up someone's physical wounds.

Caring Begins at Home

Children tend to be especially sensitive to the pain and suffering of other living creatures. In studies conducted with 300 children at the National Institute of Mental Health, it was found that as early as twelve months of age a child exhibits helping behavior—touching, patting, or some other sympathetic gesture—toward another child or an adult who appears to be in distress.[3]

If you have ever had to console a child whose puppy has been hit by a car or whose favorite goldfish has died, you know how deeply affected a young person can be. This sensitivity can be preserved, or it can be blunted. In a home where there is sympathy and concern for others, and where parents make sacrifices for those less fortunate, a child's capacity for compassion is strengthened.

Family researcher Dolores Curran says:

> Families who presume that members can and will be caring toward others become those healthy families who value service to others. They are the ones who show up in times of community need. They are there to drive the elderly, to help families clean up after floods and fire, to offer solace and food to the grief-stricken, to help old eyes prepare income tax returns, to help families move, to spring young mothers from household child care. They are just generally aware of others' needs and welfare. As the children from these families grow up, they tend to be quite caring and responsible persons as a result of their family experiences.[4]

The findings of professor David Rosenhan show that long-term devotion to the welfare of others is deeply influenced by parental models. In his study of civil rights leaders, he found that people who were only temporarily involved in the movement displayed a short-term altruism that was motivated by guilt. They dropped out. Those who stayed and went on to become leaders in the movement had parents who had exemplified for them such qualities as perseverance and courage. They had models that sustained them.[5]

When children are young, we nurture their compassionate nature by pointing out needs to which they can respond. A child can't do much to help homeless victims of a flood, but he or she can include another child in activities.

Children are helpless to do anything about war in another part of the world, but they can treat personal belongings—theirs and the property of others—with respect. A child can't do much to help the elderly who are lonely and isolated, but he or she can remember to send cards to grandparents living in distant places.

The Power of Words

The point has been made in previous chapters that our actions speak louder than our words. And never is this truer than in parenting. But that's not to discount what an important part words play in our relationships and how vital they are in carrying out our mission to love one another. Words are powerful. They can offer hope or they can discourage. They can wound or they can heal. In a given situation, we might have a choice between saying, "I respect your views," or "That's a weird idea"; between "How could you be so stupid?" or "You made a mistake. Let's see what we can do to resolve it."

Once words go forth, we're never quite sure where they will stop. Malicious gossip can destroy a reputation. But praise or a compliment can be like a stone dropped into a pond, rippling off to do good in ways we may never know. A Persian proverb says, "Blessed is he who speaks a kindness; thrice blessed is he who repeats it." If we are blessed to repeat a kindness, consider what it does for the person who gets a compliment second hand. A glow comes over people when they hear something favorable that's been said about them. This is particularly evident in children. We might tell a son that he did a good job mowing the lawn and he'll probably murmur, "Thanks." But repeat to this same boy that a neighbor said he's a hard worker who does a fine mowing job, and chances are he will smile.

Home-grown Attitudes

Children are notorious imitators, often to our embarrassment. They repeat not just our words but our tone of voice as well. Unfortunately, they also tend to carry into life any bigoted attitudes they hear at home. In an integrated neighborhood where we lived, the children in one family were continually getting into fights, most of which were racially motivated. And no wonder, when such ethnic slurs as "nigger" and "spic" were what they were used to hearing at home. Home can be either a spawning ground for prejudice and bigotry or a place where children learn tolerance and respect for those whose skin color or religion or language differs from their own.

Yet another attitude learned at home is respect—or lack of it—for the environment. Scripture reminds us that "the world and all that is in it belong to the LORD" (Psalm 24:1, TEV). Our role, then, is to be the earth's caretakers. As such, we'd do well to follow the old rule among campers that says you leave a campsite a little bit better than you found it. If this were to become an environmental philosophy, how much better and more healthful a place our planet would be! In his last speech to the United Nations, Ambassador Adlai E. Stevenson said, "We travel together, passengers on a little spaceship, dependent on its vulnerable resources of air and soil; all committed for our safety to its security and peace; preserved from annihilation only by the care, the work, and I will say, the love we give our fragile craft."[6]

There's little we, as individuals or families, can do globally about pollution and the assault on the environment, but if we're really concerned we'll do something right where we are. In our neighborhood there's a man with multiple sclerosis who is still able to go walking. On his walks he picks up pop cans and other litter. It's his small contribution to keeping the neighborhod a pleasant place to live. His concern for the environment sets a good example for his two young daughters and for those of us who are aware of his efforts. He's a reminder that caretaking is everyone's responsibility.

Good Works in Perspective

When we begin to build a family, it's important to decide what our priorities are, and then to put first things first.

Overcommitment is a problem that creeps up before we realize what's happening. It begins with good intentions when we take on some worthwhile responsibility outside the family. Over time we commit ourselves to a little more and a little more, until finally the family gets only the crumbs of our time.

I first saw this happen in the neighborhood where we lived from the mid-sixties to early seventies. It was a time of great social unrest, and the list of causes that you could be involved in got longer and longer. There were issues of integrated schools and busing, equal housing and employment opportunities, Vietnam and all the legal and moral issues it raised. Of course there were still the more traditional calls for participation in charity drives, church organizations, and the P.T.A. I felt a great pull between all of those concerns outside the home and the demands of a growing family. After attending various meetings, it became apparent that the same people showed up repeatedly. I admired their involvement and felt duly guilty when I missed a meeting about neighborhood problems or declined an invitation to march on City Hall.

But after a time, I accepted that I couldn't be all things to all people. For those who thought they could, something had to give. What I saw "giving" was the quality of their family lives. Dinner was hurried because there was an early meeting to be gotten to. Night after night, children were left with sitters who were more interested in watching TV than in attending to toddlers, more interested in doing their own homework than in reading a bedtime story to a child.

Being overcommitted isn't just a problem for parents. It happens to entire families. It's been found that healthy families value service to others, but the healthier families don't try to be active in everything from the anti-nuke movement to saving the seals. Instead they choose a single interest and focus on that.[7] Some friends of ours have as their family project an historical pioneer settlement that's a favorite local attraction. The father has been on the governing board, and the mother, along with their five children, has helped recreate the life and times of the settlement. They've hoed the corn, cleaned the restored log cabins, tended the animals, dressed in period clothing, answered visitors' questions—whatever helped maintain the settlement and keep it authentic. For this family of history buffs, it's been a unifying experience that's given them a feeling of pride in the contribution they've made to the preservation of a fine historic site.

In Giving We Receive

Those with the greatest wealth are the ones who have learned to love. And there can be no real love without reaching out to others. In giving of ourselves we store up riches of the spirit that neither time nor misfortune can take away. When home is the place where this is learned, everyone in the family has a headstart on discovering life's true riches.

Some Things to Try

- Act on needs right where you are. If you're a full-time homemaker, is there a parent in your neighborhood who has to leave for work before school opens? What a kindness it would be if the school-age child were made to feel welcome at your house! Is there an elderly person who still wants to live independently but can't handle the yard work or snow removal? What a favor it would be if a family effort were made to see that these jobs got done! Scripture tells us, " . . . blest are your eyes for they see, and your ears, for they hear" (Matthew 13:16, RSV). It's a reminder to look and listen for the needs of those around us and then to respond with love and helpfulness.
- Become part of an ecumenical network of parents that sponsors parenting-for-peace workshops. The aim of the group is to help families become more caring and give them skills with which to help others. For more information, contact:

National Parenting for Peace and Justice Network
2913 Locust
St. Louis, MO 63101

- Put yourself in the shoes of another—and ask your children to try it too. Ask: What would I want people to do for me if I were
  —confined to a wheelchair?
  —a new person on the block or new student in school?
  —grieving over the death of a loved one?
  —an old person living in a nursing home?
- Care for the environment. Recycle all the items you can, keep noise down, avoid littering, contribute to cleaner air by not smoking. Teach children a respect for nature, support legislation aimed at cleaning up toxic waste dumps and making the earth a safe and healthful place. Individual circumstances determine specific actions. Each of us doing a small part can make a big difference.
- Follow the code of the Quaker missionary Etienne de Grellet, who said, "I shall pass through this world but once. If, therefore, there be any kindness I can show, or any good thing I can do, let me do it now; let me not defer it or neglect it, for I shall not pass this way again."

Notes

Chapter 1: Deciding What You Want Home to Mean

1. Robert Coles, address delivered at Westminster Presbyterian Church, Minneapolis, January 9, 1984.
2. "Children's Questions about God Show Hunger for the Eternal," *Minneapolis Tribune*, May 6, 1984.
3. Hakon Torjesen, *The House-Husband's World* (Eden Prairie, Minnesota: The Garden, 1979).
4. "Study Shows Home Background Is Top Factor in Education," *New York Times* Service, *Minneapolis Tribune*, May 25, 1973.
5. David Elkind, *The Hurried Child* (Reading, Massachusetts: Addison-Wesley, 1981).
6. Morris Mandel, *The Jewish Press*. Reprinted in *Reader's Digest*, "Points to Ponder," August 1983.

Chapter 2: Building Self-Esteem

1. John Powell, *Fully Human, Fully Alive* (Niles, Illinois: Argus Communications, 1976).
2. Thomas Lickona, *Raising Good Children* (New York: Bantam Books, 1983).
3. David Elkind, "Growing Up Faster," *Psychology Today*, February 1979.
4. Lickona, op. cit.
5. Haim Ginott, *Between Parent and Child* (New York: Avon, 1965).
6. Mary Wilke, ed. Michael Gecan, *Seen Through Our Eyes* (New York: Random House, 1972).
7. Lillian Katz, address delivered at Early Childhood Conference, St. Norbert's College, West De Pere, Wisconsin, April 17, 1984.

Chapter 3: Taking Time for Your Family

1. David P. O'Neill, *What Do You Say to a Child When You Meet a Flower?* (St. Meinrad, Indiana: Abbey Press, 1972).

2. Patrick Boley, "What Was Your Favorite Toy?" *Minneapolis Star and Tribune*, April 10, 1984.
3. Ann Blackman, "These Mothers Stay Home, Take Pride in It," Associated Press, *Minneapolis Tribune*, November 4, 1984.
4. Miriam Winterbottom, *The Christian Science Monitor* News Service. Reprinted in the *Minneapolis Tribune*, August 10, 1978.
5. "Study: Dad Can Help Child Be Better Student," *New York Times* Service, *Minneapolis Tribune*, November 4, 1976.
6. John M. Drescher, *If I Were Starting My Family Over Again* (Nashville: Abingdon, 1979).

Chapter 4: Listening with Your Heart

1. O'Neill, op. cit. (see ch. 3, n. 1).
2. Don Dinkmeyer and Gary D. McKay, *The Parent's Handbook* (Circle Pines, Minnesota: American Guidance Service, 1982).
3. *Suicide in Youth and What You Can Do about It* (San Mateo, California: Suicide Prevention and Crisis Center, n.d.).
4. *Youth and Suicide* (Weymouth, Massachusetts: Life Skills Education, 1983).
5. "Prayer of the Christophers," *Christopher News Notes*, May 1978.

Chapter 5: Making TV a Creative Force

1. *TV or Not TV, a Vacuum in the Tube* (Cincinnati, Ohio: Pamphlet Publications, 1978).
2. *Fighting TV Stereotypes* (Newtonville, Massachusetts: Action for Children's Television Handbook, 1983).
3. "Influence of TV Rated at Top in Youth Survey," Associated Press, *Minneapolis Tribune*, January 5, 1976.
4. *Fighting TV Stereotypes*, op. cit.
5. *TV or Not TV, a Vacuum in the Tube*, op. cit.
6. G. B. Richardson, "Sophisticated Babies," *Reader's Digest*, February 1984.
7. *Fighting TV Stereotypes*, op. cit.
8. *Young Families* (University of Minnesota Agricultural Extension Service, November-December 1977).
9. *Window Dressing on the Set: An Update* (Report by the U.S. Commission on Civil Rights, 1979).
10. Ibid.

Chapter 6: Discovering the Power of Prayer

1. Wirt and Beckstrom, *Living Quotations for Christians* (New York: Harper and Row, 1974).
2. Alexis Carrel, *Reflections on Life* (New York: Hawthorn Books, 1952).
3. Norman Vincent Peale, *Treasury of Courage and Confidence* (Anderson, Indiana: Warner Press, 1970).
4. Lew Miller, *Your Divine Connection* (Milbrae, California: Celestial Arts, 1977).
5. "Finishing First, at Last," *Time*, August 13, 1984.
6. Peter Marshall, *Mr. Jones, Meet the Master* (Old Tappan, New Jersey: Fleming H. Revell, 1949).
7. Ardis Whitman, "Six Special Powers of Prayer," *Reader's Digest*, April 1980.
8. Brigadier General and Mrs. James A. Dozier, "A Story of Answered Prayer," *Guideposts*, January 1983.
9. Alfred Lord Tennyson, *Morte d'Arthur*.

Chapter 7: Growing into a Faith

1. John E. Corrigan, *Growing Up Christian* (Dayton, Ohio: Pflaum/Standard Publishing, 1969).
2. Benjamin Spock, "What to Tell Your Child about God," *Redbook*, August 1978.
3. Margot Slade, "When the Firstborn Comes, Religion Is Often Reborn," *New York Times* Service, *Minneapolis Tribune*, June 10, 1984.
4. Adapted from Dolores Curran, *In the Beginning There Were Parents* (Minneapolis: Winston Press, 1978).
5. Lickona, op. cit. (see ch. 2, n. 2).

Chapter 8: Forgiving and Forgetting

1. "Milestones," *Time*, February 27, 1984.
2. Wirt and Beckstrom, op. cit. (see ch. 6, n. 1).
3. Norman Vincent Peale, op. cit. (see ch. 6, n. 3).
4. "Burglar Rewards Self by Making Restitution," Associated Press, *Minneapolis Tribune*, November 11, 1976.
5. "Newspaper Ad Apology Helps Ease Burden of 46 Years," Associated Press, *Minneapolis Tribune*, June 16, 1984.

6. "Parents Win Mercy for Drunken Driver Who Killed Their Son," Associated Press, *Minneapolis Tribune*, December 17, 1983.
7. Catherine Marshall, *Something More* (New York: McGraw-Hill, 1974).
8. "I Spoke . . . As a Brother," *Time*, January 9, 1984.

Chapter 9: Keeping Christ in Christmas

1. Robert T. Smith column, *Minneapolis Tribune*, December 14, 1977.

Chapter 11: Doing Something About Hunger

1. "Hunger Quiz," Hunger Action Coalition, 310 East 38th Street, Minneapolis, Minnesota 55409.
2. Robert Hutchinson, *What One Christian Can Do about Hunger in America* (Chicago: Fides/Claretian, 1982).
3. Jerome Boxleitner, *Newsletter*, Catholic Charities of the Archdiocese of St. Paul and Minneapolis, Spring 1984.
4. "Hunger Quiz," op. cit.
5. NBC Feature on Hunger, 6 O'clock News, May 10, 1984.
6. Hutchinson, op. cit.
7. Ibid.
8. "Hunger Quiz," op. cit.
9. *The Hunger Times* (Minneapolis: The American Lutheran Church, 1982-83).
10. "Hunger Quiz," op. cit.
11. *The Hunger Times*, op. cit.
12. Ibid.

Chapter 12: Touching with Love

1. Frederick Leboyer, *Loving Hands* (New York: Knopf, 1976).
2. Ashley Montagu, *Touching: The Human Significance of the Skin* (New York: Columbia University Press, 1971).
3. Ibid.
4. Helen Colton, *The Gift of Touch* (New York: Putnam, 1983).
5. Arthur Janov, "For Control, Cults Must Ease the Most Profound Pains," *Los Angeles Times*, December 10, 1978.
6. Jules Older, *Touching Is Healing* (Briarcliff Manor, New York: Stein and Day, 1982).

7. Leo Buscaglia, *Love* (New York: Fawcett Crest, 1972).
8. Sally Cooper, "Confronting a Near and Present Danger," *Ms.*, April 1984.
9. "Sexual Abuse of Children," *Minneapolis Tribune*, January 1, 1984.
10. Ibid., January 4, 1984.
11. Older, op. cit.

Chapter 13: Accepting Death as a Part of Life

1. *TV or Not TV, a Vacuum in the Tube*, op. cit. (see ch. 5, n. 1).
2. Ginott, op. cit. (see ch. 2, n. 5).
3. Marc Wilson, "Death Education Crucial for Children," Associated Press, *Minneapolis Star*, December 17, 1977.
4. Lynn Caine, *Widow* (New York: William Morrow, 1974).
5. Elisabeth Kübler-Ross, *Death the Final Stage of Growth* (Englewood Cliffs, New Jersey: Prentice-Hall, 1975).

Chapter 14: Going Forth

1. Viktor E. Frankl, *Man's Search for Meaning* (New York: Washington Square Press, 1963).
2. "Saints Among Us," *Time*, December 25, 1975.
3. Joel Greenberg, "Why Does Anyone Help Another? 'Happy People Give So Much More,'" *New York Times* Service, *Minneapolis Tribune*, July 19, 1981.
4. Dolores Curran, *Traits of a Healthy Family* (Minneapolis: Winston Press, 1983).
5. Greenberg, op. cit.
6. *Christopher News Notes*, October 1975.
7. Curran, op. cit.